THE GOSPEL
SITS AT MY BREAKFAST TABLE

DAVID B. LOVEALL

David and Nita Loveall's story about their tireless quest to adopt a boy from Uganda is full of grit and grace, laughter and tears, hope and despair. Above all, it is a story of faith played out not in the cozy confines of some living-room Bible study but in the raw and risky streets of the real world, its ending a tear-stained manifestation of Oswald Chambers' admonition for us to live with "reckless joy."

BOB WELCH, speaker, author, award-winning columnist and teacher.

An amazing story about an even more amazing boy's journey...all starting with a mother's promise. Words like interesting, engaging and entertaining don't do this story justice. Trust me.

STEPHANIE HOFFMAN, former University of Oregon track thrower, mom of two college-bound athletes.

Every reader will get an up close view of how the Gospel once entreated, beautifully works its way out of the human soul. The Loveall's relentless pursuit of the heart of God through simple obedience paints a vivid picture of the Father's pursuit of broken humanity. At first glance we might only see that William had everything to gain, but upon closer inspection, we see the Loveall's literally transformed by this selfless act of love. In essence a beautiful mosaic is weaved together from the threads of their very different lives as the grace of God invades their souls. May we all invite Jesus into our lives in the way the Loveall's have demonstrated...We change the world one act of obedience motivated by love, toward one person at a time.

KEITH "PK" JENKINS, Pastor and Visionary, New LifeLA church.

THE GOSPEL SITS AT MY BREAKFAST TABLE

Requests for information should be address to:
Three Sixteen Ministries Int'l
david@threesixteenministries.com

ISBN-13: 978-1516961139 CreateSpace, a DBA of On-Demand Publishing, LLC.
ISBN-10: 1516961137
BISAC: Biography & Autobiography / Personal Memoirs

This is the story of our adoption of William Biyinzika Loveall. A young Ugandan orphan who made a powerful prayer to God that unbeknownst to my wife, stole her heart while she was on a mission trip. Over the next two years, this impossible prayer turned our "empty nest" life, into a story larger than we ever imagined. It also brought a deeper, more personal understanding of what being adopted into Christ means for all of us. The name "Biyinzika" means all things are possible, including the impossible.

Cover and Interior design: Bethany Loveall, JULY NINE.com
Cover and inset photos: Loveallphoto.com
First Printing March 2016 / Printed in the U.S.A.

THE GOSPEL
SITS AT MY BREAKFAST TABLE

by David B. Loveall

Dedicated to the unknown lady-angel who slid the forty dollars across my wife's work counter and said "go." The value of that confirmation set all of these and countless other events in motion. What you thought was miniature generosity has touched and changed thousands of lives. You will never know this side of heaven what those two twenty-dollar bills did in the kingdom of eternity, but your legacy, like good fruit, will always remain.

Wherever you rest now, rest assured, you answered a mighty calling, which in turn, raised up so many to do the same.

Not bad for forty bucks.

TABLE OF CONTENTS

EPILOGUE

ACKNOWLEDGEMENTS

1

THE VISION

Dreams. Visions. Biyinzika.

From the top of the hill, Jireh Children's Orphanage in Uganda had a million-dollar view, and a million reasons why a young man would struggle to dream.

William routinely gazed over the valleys below. There was always a thin layer of campfire cooking smoke from those preparing daily meals, which served as a constant reminder to the fragile struggle of life in Africa. Also hovering with the haze was the even leaner, heavier layer of limited potential. A smoky, bulletproof ceiling, smothering even the slightest hope that any other life could exist, other than one of hand-to-mouth survival.

What kind of dreams is a young boy in a Ugandan orphanage capable of dreaming? He sees the facts and, like many wide-eyed innocent children tries to find something that could someday be transformed into hope, but there's always that reminder of the suffocating smoke. Along with the 200 other kids around him, daily hope consisted of a meager meal of Posho mash and beans served on a worn plastic plate. It was a testament to the sameness and familiarity unequally coupled with the uncertainty that loomed just ahead of all of them, when they would either enter high school if funds were found, or be kicked onto the streets.

His birth father, rumored to have been killed in a car accident when William was four, left his mother without a safety net in the mazes of Kampala. Unmarried and unemployed, she tried to open and run a small produce store in the slums, but she was barely able to care for herself and look after her own safety, much less care for the needs of a small boy.

Within a short period of time, a man of a different faith laid claim to his desires for her, and she remarried. At first, that might have looked like a silver lining, but instead it was one more setback in a series to follow. In the new husband's faith, adopting the children of the previous mate was not automatic. In fact, on religious grounds, he refused.

There were relatives three hours to the west in the villages about 30 kilometers outside Masaka. Good Catholics, they had meager homes and were occasionally employed. William's mother put him on a bus to live with his grandparents in a tiny, mud-bricked hut surrounded by banana fields. But that too, proved temporary. Too many mouths to feed and too few resources.

He was handed over to his mom's oldest sister, who lived in town and ran a business. She took him in for a while, but with her seamstress wages and the demands of her own kids, she couldn't keep the basics of life stitched together with the added burden of William.

Up the road in the hills, the oldest sister found Jireh, an orphanage/school that didn't charge the traditional school fees like most of the other boarding facilities. Jireh means, "the Lord provides," and she convinced the caretakers to take him in. Now twelve years old, William had been at the orphanage since he was six.

Jireh literally sits atop a king's hill. It is leased from the local provincial king and got it's start from a Christian pastor whose desire was to extend the hand of God to care for orphans. It later partnered with a Christian group from America, US2Uganda4Life, and for the past number of years, the children and the care of the facility have been a focal point for annual mission trips coming from America.

Over the years, young William had developed into somewhat of a leader and an ambassador to the steady stream of "Muzungu"-white visitors. "You have a strong gift for relationships and it's obvious that you have God's favor upon you," the Jireh pastor told him.

Many subsequent church groups came and went, making emotional promises to stay in contact and to send help, but, just like the Muzungu promises, nothing ever came of those momentary assurances.

A child raised on such false hope might slink into bitterness and distrust, but if there was one thing that living at Jireh taught William, it was the power of provision and the waiting on a promise. To the outsider, daily life may have looked like last-minute planning or crisis management, as supplies, food, and clothing needs were haphazardly scraped together on a monthly donation basis. But to the children, this was proof of God's promise to provide. They had food when they needed it. They had a school. They had a place to sleep, a sense of community, and their own little private spot to look over the valley with the million-dollar view, and dream of a time when the smoke of obscurity might clear.

William remembers the moment when that happened for him. It was a vision, or maybe even a daydream somewhere between the veil of consciousness and blatant reality. A thought so grand and so incomprehensible that his friends laughed at him when he shared it.

It was a vision that he not only would have the funds to go to high school, but that high school would be in a far-off land.

America.

It was an unlikely vision, the kind an orphan boy in the village of Masaka, atop a hill in a facility that not many know even exists, really has no business believing. To think of the hows and the whos would be a depth of imagination no one could fathom. Indeed, the thought alone would seemingly trigger others to laugh, if not hold the boy up to public humiliation.

But somehow, under that boyhood face, shaved head, and baggy pants, young William developed a man-sized plan. He looked at his habits and decided he needed to change. He fasted. For three solid days he went without food. Who does that at twelve? He re-energized his worship. He flushed out doubts when they would come to the surface of "reality." His prayers were pointed and punchy. And his name, he decided, needed to change.

"My last name meant nothing (Kyambadde), and that nothing was something not very good, because it hadn't led anywhere," he said.

William remembered a few biblical names he had learned from boarding school teachers, three men whose names were changed by God to prepare them to embark on their visions: Abram became Abraham, who set off to settle in a land not knowing how or where; Jacob became Israel, who became the leader of God's nation; and Simon became Peter, the brash and independent fisherman, the rock.

All of them developed new character by a name which shaped them for a new future. William observed that they were all empowered by their new names, like archers' arrows being aimed at new targets. If he were to have any chance at all, William decided, he needed not only a new target. He needed to be a new arrow.

He changed his name, from "nothing" to "Biyinzika," after an older girl who had recently left Jireh to attend high school across town. In Africa, it's customary to say the last name first, so from that moment forward he lived as the newly adopted name meant. At twelve years young, Biyinzika William entered the seventh grade, the level just before high school, with an entirely different promise.

"Biyinzika" means "all things possible."

2

TWO-BILL CONFIRMATION

"Consecrate yourselves for tomorrow the Lord will do amazing things among you."
Joshua 3:5 NLT

Back in America, forty dollars slid across a dental office counter. The donation was as if God were writing new characters into Biyinzika William's dream sequence.

The buzz and whir of the instruments barely overtook that definitive smell of my wife's dental office being chill-forced through the floor vents. That particular August afternoon the air conditioning was having a hard time keeping up with the heat of her empty-nester hot flashes. She had been a hygienist at this office since the last week of pregnancy with our daughter—who is now married and graduated from college.

As a hygienist in the old mill town of Springfield, Oregon, she typically has a handful of sharp tools and a captive audience of one. Seven times a day in her chair, each patient would be tipped back and attuned to the voice behind the blue mask.

One day in that summer of 2011, a particular patient was an elderly retired widow, somewhere between social security and surviving. A soft-spoken, homey, grandma-type who you could trust with the secrets of a pie recipe. And yet in the twenty-three years Nita had worked in the office, the woman had never been in before. She was a virtual drop in.

The crinkly paper was pinned about her neck. The weathered, but manicured fingertips nervously tapped delicately on the ends of the armrest. The routine began like clockwork with the standard questions as the volume of the gurgle and sucking sounds kicked in.

"How are you doing today?," a kindly voice from behind the starched paper of protection asks.

The answer is usually benignly brief.

"Any changes to your health? Anything you would like the dentist to know about at the end of your appointment?"

That said, Nita has always considered that more is going on in these brief relationships than mere dental stuff.

"Life happens in my chair: death, major events, people downloading on me," she said. "Most of the time, it's nothing about dentistry and so much about everything else."

"It's ordinary work, for sure, but it's more. It's sucking spit and polishing teeth on the onset, but it moves quickly into ministry, counseling and listening to dramatic stories, changes in relationships, kids growing up. Then it's back to simpler concepts, like convincing people which end of the toothbrush to use."

At the time, Nita was wrestling with the request of a long-time friend from California, Mary, a retired hygienist, to go to Uganda. Specifically a place called Jireh as part of a mission team. The plan was to go to the orphanage and assess dental needs and do any necessary treatment for a couple of weeks. It's something Nita had done in Romania, Mexico, and other parts of the world.

The no-vote had plenty of supporters: Lack of money and time away from family for starters.

"There are 100 reasons why I can't go to Africa," Nita said to her patient after sharing the possibility of the trip with her. “I would have to try and fund-raise about $3,000, which would require me to send out those silly ‘would-you-sponsor-me?’ letters. I hate asking people. And there doesn’t seem to be enough time to get all that done in the next month and a half before they leave.”

The cleaning instruments prohibited a lot of immediate comebacks as one might expect, but between rinsing and suctioning, the soft-spoken grandmother was listening—and thinking how she could help.

Nita finished the final chicken scratches into the chart pages and shepherded the slow-moving woman back to the receptionist. Like thousands of patients before her, she was digging into her purse, perhaps to find her keys or checkbook or bifocals to see the billing information that was about to be scooted across the front counter

Just as the widow turned to leave, she stepped close to my wife and leaned on the granite divider between the lobby and the receptionist.

“I’ve always dreamed of doing what you’re doing but I’m too old now,” she said.

Her eyes were full of emotion, brimming, as if being pulled into a story greater than herself.

“I’m going to live this experience through you,” she said and slid two twenty-dollar bills across the counter. “This is for your trip.”

She smiled and slipped out the door.

Nita took a blank letter-sized envelope from the slot near the front computer. She tucked the bills inside it and wrote one word across the front in bold black ink: Africa.

The smooth concreted floor bounced math concepts and English lessons from the painted blackboard to the students seated in rough hewn wooden desks. The chalk and red clay dust clung on every ledge, contrasted with clean slate blue workbooks stacked neatly at the end of each row. Daily study routines mirrored the sun: up and ready early; till dark. The walls were bright yellow, peppered with waist-high dirty handprints.

Seventh grade was coming to a close; it was test time. High school was just a few months away. For Biyinzika William's vision, it was crunch time.

He seized his pencil with disciplined vigor as he had done nearly everyday before. Math. History. Science. English. He scratched each answer carefully into his test booklet. The instructor's gait was catlike to any whispers. "Eyes on your own work," he would say as he circled around the room.

Testing results are a big deal in Uganda. The results from varying districts are all published in a special edition newspaper for everyone to see and compare. Headlines would blast in war-like font, "What school was the best?" "Which student holds the most promise?" "How high were the scores in your area?" Each subject was graded separately and then a total performance score would be awarded. From that total, it determined the next course of action for each student. Trade school? College? Or the school of hard-knocks, the streets.

When the results were made public, the motorcycle taxi drivers were unusually inattentive to the waving of potential customers and service was slower, from the woman behind the café counter to the coffin maker along the main road, who sat on a wooden box pouring over the results.

A few schools in Jireh's Masaka region had done extremely well that year, in fact better than ever. People boasted of village kids finally getting the trickle-down education that the nation had hoped for. So much expectation. So much excitement. All about to expire like a party balloon popped.

If Uganda had a middle name, it would be corruption. It's not so much a moral issue as it is a way of survival. From lower level governmental officials on down to the local street vendor, prestige and honor speak volumes about a person's identity. But in a pinch, and for a certain amount of shillings, it can be bought.

The examiners, it was discovered, had cooked the scores to reflect better achievement. It was a move solely designed to benefit themselves, but the punishment would ripple beyond—to the students.

The educational minister determined that, as punishment, every student under each of the deceptive directors would have to repeat the grade they had just finished. The celebration of just weeks ago was now collective grumble, a colossal setback for everyone.

Except for Biyinzika William.

"High school was just a few months away and nothing had happened that whole year toward the vision," he said shrugging off the delay. "I knew at that moment it was God telling me that the vision was certain. I had no doubt. I was going to America for high school. It was a celebration for me."

Nita had her forty dollars seed money and quickly raised the remainder from sponsorships and cracking down on the family eating out budget. She was ready to go to Uganda in record time.

William had his setback. He was ready to go America.

3

PIERCING THE HEART

"And God will wipe away every tear from their eyes; there shall be no more death, nor sorrow, nor crying. There shall be no more pain, for the former things have passed away."

Revelation 21:4 NKJ

Three rotten teeth were the tariff for the heart of Nita.

While Biyinzika William's mouth throbbed daily with the pain of the three molars, the last plane from Amsterdam descended over the moonlight reflections from Lake Victoria as it approached the Entebbe airport.

On board: Mary, her lifelong friend from California, 22 college students and a handful of medical staffer adults. Each trying to shake the 30 hours of coach compartment travel as best they could. They loaded into a couple of Toyota beater trucks and, with Jireh pastors at the wheels, disappeared into the dark diesel fog to the nearby overnight hotel.

The town of Masaka was a treacherous three-hour drive on a two lane highway, mostly un-striped, choked with boda-bodas (motorcycle taxis) carrying passengers, chickens, produce, and too many people. It was a recipe for vehicular disaster.

Between gasps and the treacherous vehicle tipping around the corners, Nita and Mary tried to take their minds off the peril, instead focusing on the upcoming ten days of dental intervention. They had planned and brought instruments to do what they knew, which was cleaning somewhat healthy teeth, applying fluoride, putting sealants on top of molars to prevent decay, reminding people to floss, and giving outgoing happy patients sugar-free gum.

But there's a saying on the Dark Continent: "T.I.A." "This is Africa." Which means "normal" is that anything and everything always goes sideways. A person's best laid plans aren't plans at all, they're feeble attempts at pushing the Nile River backwards. Power outages. Slow-moving people with no concept of time. Nothing turns out as you had planned. Nothing.

"We went to do what we call normal, preventative dentistry," Nita said. "You know, cleaning and tooth sealants and for some reason we brought an old sterilizer that Mary got from a warehouse donation that houses retired equipment. We had some room in the checked bags and thought we might use it or trade the unit for something else of value."

Then the T.I.A. factor drilled its way in like a bad abscess.

"On arrival to Jireh we were greeted by these lovely, happy, singing, smiling children, but quickly we noticed some things that made all our plans go out the window," she said.

"What we found at Jireh, upon an initial exam out in the playground, was 14 children and two staff members who were in moderate to severe pain. Our plan then went from routine treatment to triage. We needed to find a dentist fast and extract the teeth. I hated that option, and I felt bad about doing it, but it was all we could do. These all were potentially serious cases."

Having no tools for the surgical requirements and not much anesthetic packed, the options got slim until the pastor's wife located a local dentist who would trade services at her treatment center for something she needed—a sterilizer. Go figure.

Six of the kids in serious pain were randomly picked and, along with one one adult, jalopied down the hill to the local town of Masaka. Songs swathed the van like the red dust along the way, led by the two blond hygienists hanging on for dear life to the seat piping.

"We sort of unified the two countries with singing," Nita remembers. "The song 'if-you're-happy-and-you-know-it-clap-your-hands' was a big hit, and we shouted it over and over. It took their minds off the pain and the uncertainty of what was about to happen. They just trusted us and got into a van and said 'OK'."

The clinic was rugged, to say the least. Dingy white walls, weathered wood benches and about a meter up the wall, a brown smudge stripe blotted in by the backs of the previous patients' heads. One bare bulb light in the middle, hanging from two wires supplied the waiting room ambience and the next fire hazard. Behind the entry wall, the exam room, two prehistoric metal chairs, complete with web straps, one tube of fluorescent illumination, a window and a shelf of instruments, circa 1950.

Mary and Nita paused for a few moments to stuff the impending emotional burp and abruptly kicked into "professional" mode.

This was tooth pulling in its most basic sense, tools cleansed only by disinfectant wipes. T.I.A. On the first two patients, the doctor reached in with pliers, and like she had done apparently many times before, grabbed the top of the tooth and sharply broke off the crown. Right at the gum line. She proceeded to dig the remaining root tips out like the locals shovel up yams. Mary could hardly contain herself.

"I just softly blurted out, 'in America we always try to get the tooth and the roots out all in one piece,'" Mary said, still squirming from the memory. "It was just so barbaric and those poor little kids suffering all that unnecessary trauma."

She said the doctor looked up as if given an epiphany and in a heavy accent mumbled, "I've never considered that before." She finished digging out the root tips of patient number three and was ready to give the new technique a college try on the next.

His name was Biyinzika William.

He was Jireh's "big-little man on campus" and was visibly terrified. The looks and paralysis of his friends before him had petrified him. Those same eyes were scanning the room for any bits of comfort or reassurance.

"As usual, I would talk each kid through the procedure," Nita said. "I wasn't the one pulling the teeth so I could pull their attention away from the cracking and harvesting sounds and the unusual feeling of numbness none of them had ever felt before. They trusted us, as adults and as Americans. I was determined to get each of them through the process."

William crept into the prehistoric chair, surrendered to whatever was to come. His friends and bunkmates, gauze stuffed into their blood-splotched mouths, spoke like they were affected by some paralyzing spirit. The anxiety was building.

Nita realized Biyinzika William's fear. "It's OK to be afraid," she said. "You keep looking and listening to me, and I promise I will get you through this. You can trust me."

How many times had people in his life said that, only to have their actions reveal an empty promise? Still, for some reason, he reached out and gripped Nita's hand. He trusted her.

He had three teeth that were on the verge of a full-blown puss festival. They were all adult teeth and regrettably, they all had to go. Long roots, far in the back. This was going to be a dental battle.

"I will get you through this," Nita said again, squeezing his hand.

After the second tooth was out, a tear ran down his cheek. Nita wiped it with a clean gauze pad. After the third, she clutched his little-boy cheeks.

"Great job!" she said. "Even though you were afraid, you were brave. I'm proud of you and you should be proud of you, too."

She gave him a "mamma-type" hug, partially one of relief and certainly one of triumph. A bashful smile stretched across William's anesthetized face. It was a tender moment, but the clock was ticking, more patients were waiting. The two missionary hygienists shifted to the next gear, game-on to the next mouth.

As Nita looked back on that afternoon, she still couldn't have noticed what deep extractions in her were taking place too. Maybe she was too masked into "the professional," too much on automatic, too much in the depths of work mode to notice. But something was stirring inside her.

4

THE SORRY SONG PROMISE

"That which has gone from your lips you shall keep and perform. For you voluntarily made a vow with the Lord your God what you have promised with your mouth."
Deuteronomy 23:23 NKJ

A letter, a song of gratitude and a promise.

It started with a letter of thanks and grew to the largest promise she had ever made.

Scribbled onto a sheet of folded paper, the edge bearing the signature rip from a tattered school workbook, were the carefully penned English words. The lines were semi-straight despite being written not only in the dark, but from a boy with an aching mouth.

The note had been personally delivered to Nita that next day, tendered to her as if a notice from royalty. She put one arm around him and began to read the carefully written piece. The note began as most Muzungus are addressed, dear "auntie" or "uncle" a title representing both affection and respect.

"Dear my friend Aunt Anina,
How are you and how is your life? For me I am fine because I am still alive. The main reason why I have written this letter is to thank you for the love

you have shown and the treatment you have given me.

I know that you have become my everlasting friend because it's not easy for someone to treat you without payment. But you, you did it and I know that even God is going to pay you. So I am very happy for that.

May God Bless you. From William B."

From the locals' perspective, it's expected that visiting missionaries are coming to provide service. Unfortunately, what's started to trickle down is that Muzungus are also a ready source of money. Getting a hand inside an American pocket is like getting the Willie Wonka golden ticket. So many missionaries pass through Uganda on a fairly regular basis now that children who would have never thought to cross cultural lines of disrespect, now boldly ask for school sponsorships, extra clothes, even blatant hand-outs of cash. This is where real, honest gratitude starts to get muddled, which is why this letter was so unusual.

It resembles the biblical ten-leper story who shout from afar their desire for Jesus to instantly heal them. These ten men hadn't a hope in Hades to be restored healthily to their families or community; they were, by all means, the walking dead. However, Jesus heals them on the spot, but only one guy returns to thank Him and pay some gratitude. From this one guy, Jesus then instructs him to go and show himself to the priest, thus authenticating the miracle throughout the community. This bore witness that indeed, Heaven had come to earth.

Gratitude does that. It bears witness that Christ is in the neighborhood, and in the people.

It's quite possible that this thankful leper may have also had a vision. A vision that some day he would be healed and restored to a different life. But if he had, he kept it to himself, just as William did. He wasn't asking for anything from anyone, nor hedging a bet against the promise he clung to. He just wanted to say thanks.

William hurried off, late for class. Tears in her eyes, Nita turned to Mary. "Oh my God, I think that kid just stole my heart."

Temporary theft of the heart isn't uncommon in the mission field. However, it usually gets drowned out with the tasks at hand and the fact that fully taking on the plight of an orphan is just out of the question.

This story, however, goes beyond "usually."

For the next week and a half, when he wasn't in class, William was a near constant companion to Nita. He would help with carrying supplies, translate instructions to patients, ping-pong questions about America, and sit beside her on bus rides to soccer games.

Once, when I mistakenly called Nita instead of free-texting her, I heard an unfamiliar and uncomfortable voice.

"This is Auntie Nita's phone, William speaking." Shocked that anyone would have possession of such a coveted device, I was nearly speechless.

"Who is this?" I asked.

"This is Biyinsika William," he said. "Is this Uncle David?"

"No this is *not* Uncle David. Who are you again and what have you done with my wife?"

I felt as if I was about to be ripped off by a Nigerian con-man. But after I heard Nita laugh a few times in the background I relaxed—a little.

"Hey, you be the man there who looks after and takes care of my treasured wife," I said. "And be a good man of integrity." I'm not sure why I said the integrity part, but he assured me my Nita was in good hands. He promised he would do his best.

Nita had gained more than a buddy and certainly more than just a personal assistant. There were some deeper spiritual attachment at work because every message and text from her spoke of him. Still, I thought little more about the boy, oblivious to the idea that the Almighty was about to push one of us over the edge of the cliff, heart first.

For Nita, it was time to say goodbye. The women of Jireh prepared lunch for all of the visitors over a fire. The workers, students, and mission trip adults gathered for the traditional group meal and African departure songs. A handful of children performed skits, danced and clapped gleeful vocals while some of the boys pounded tribal beats on cow-skinned drums.

Everything was upbeat until the "I'm sorry, so sorry" song. In choral concerto the children formed a line as they clapped out the cries of their hearts. One by one, they stepped forward to a special Muzungu buddy, auntie, or uncle, and sang the delicate words to the song of departure.

"Sorry, so sorry, soon you will be leaving, soon you will be leaving. What am I to do? What am I to do?"

Having experienced songs like this in other countries on other mission trips, it was easier for Nita to be one step away from a group of people than one step away from Biyinzika William. He was the last to step forward. He was the oldest, and the supposedly more mature, and now the most maudlin.

"I'm so sorry, so sorry". He sang—or tried to sing. All Nita heard among his second-line blubbering was, "What will I do"?

It was the first time he had ever cried. I guess of all the people who had come before, Auntie Nita was the one who showed more love than all the others.

Nita's tears matched his. "Oh my God, what shall I do?" she said to herself. The entire group of visiting Muzungus was so overtaken by the final verse that yelps of emotion busted through the chanting of the children.

Nita broke away from the sitting bench and came around the table. She put her arm around his quaking shoulders and through the noise put her lips to his ears. "I will return," she said. "I promise."

The promise had not been made nonchalantly. "I knew I couldn't make an empty promise to him," she said. "In our family, a promise is something you keep, even if your life depends on it. Realistically, I figured I was promising to come back for the next US2UGANDA4LIFE trip. Check up on him, or help him with school fees, maybe in a year or so."

She explained to William that it would be a great challenge and committed to work extra hard, save the money it would require, so she could come back, and see him again. It was a promise he had heard before. But something about her was different.

"I know you will," he said.

He didn't know why he was so confident. He only knew that he loved her more than anyone who had come before. Nor did he think for a moment that Nita was part of the fulfillment of his prayer. Nor did he ask.

He thanked her again for helping him and watched her get on the bus. Nita watched him stand by himself, disconnected from the crowd but connected to her in almost a tunnel vision sort of way. All of the sounds and commotions silenced in the solitary stare of one boy.

He never waved goodbye.

Early the next morning, right before departure, one of the guys had to run an errand back to Jireh. Nita could see William one last time, but she opted not to. She had already promised to return, and, besides, her insides were already torn up enough.

After Nita left, William settled back into the routine of prayer and fasting for the vision he received. He prayed not for a single person to bring him to America, but just for a good, God-fearing family to welcome him in.

Such a family was already considering as much—all because of a boy's simple note of simple gratitude.

5

THE SEASON OF ANGUISH

When I worked as a photojournalist, I used to process images in the darkroom. It required three steps. First, the developer, which would bring out the image, then the stop bath, the solution that would halt the action, and finally, the fixer, the final step that would make the image fade proof.

Now, on our refrigerator was an image that, to Nita and me, seemed fade proof. It was a photo of William talking on the cell phone to me while Nita was at Jireh. His smile was bright, his slightly swollen cheeks glowing with glee. And it was as if his spirit had suddenly transported itself right into our kitchen and sparked a sudden dose of insanity.

I was doing dishes while Nita sat at the breakfast bar. The kitchen faucet was running along with my mouth—both mindless apparently. The topic of the discussion escapes me now, but the instantaneous reaction to the build-up of unnecessary running drinking water is still crystal clear.

Suddenly, like a defensive back trying to intercept a pass, Nita lunged for the faucet and shut off the water. She then offered some smack-talk about kids in Africa who don't have enough water. And then about how kids don't have enough money to finish school and how kids like

William don't have anything to fall back on and would eventually end up on the streets. Or dead. She was becoming an emotional wreck.

"Does this mean you don't want the dishes done?" I asked sheepishly. "Or do you want me to catch the run-off and box it up for the kids in Uganda?"

Mission-trip PTSD happens every time someone goes on one. The world of what's important and valuable gets rocked off kilter by the sharp severity of poverty and need, contrasted by a level of joy while surrounded with virtually nothing. PTSD further sets in when travelers collide with their previous lives, which look increasingly marred by insignificance.

Nita and I've both been there from countless trips to other countries. I even remember the time when I last saw this same out-of-body look on her. We were in the mountains of Bolivia, near Lake Titicaca on a trip with Compassion International. Nita was holding a chapped-cheeked baby swaddled in woven wool in a stiff mountain breeze, the fifth child of a poor high mountain family. "Sorry, honey," I said. "But at customs, I hear they still check your bags. It's impossible to even think about it."

"But what will happen to this one?" she pleaded.

"We are helping, that's why we are here, doing the best we can," I said. "We will bring back the message, people will help, they will in turn get on board with support and in the process, help this one, and hopefully many more."

And that's a frame of mind most people who engage in mission trips just learn to live with. It's a process with restrictions and red tape. You can visit, you can help, you can hurt for sure, and you can educate others in the plight. But unfortunately it starts to end up feeling like the zoo, feeding them is fine, but you just can't take 'em home.

With time, though, you either slip back into your old ways, forgetting all the idle self promises made in the emotional moment of the experiences, or somehow find a balance in keeping perspective on life here. The rare third choice is answering a mysterious call from God. Wrestling ensues. Either you surrender and follow, or fight it until it becomes an empty hole of avoidance. Either way, it turns your life—and anybody who happens to be in the way—upside down.

I know. It was happening before my eyes.

Months had passed since Nita had come back from the mountaintop orphanage. The tales of Jireh Children's Center were on her lips nearly every day as various dental patients caught up with the six-month check-up-cycle heard the news. There was the retold story of the lady with forty dollars, the traumas of young kids losing adult teeth to save their lives from infection, power outages and bathroom humor. Above all, there was this detailed account of a young boy named Biyinsika William. Every time his name was mentioned, there was emotion and unrelenting tears. We had the Costco-sized tissue boxes in every room of the house. I started to believe I could nearly do the dishes with the liquid from those tears.

"Hey, honey, what's with the water works every time you talk about this kid?" I asked countless times.

Her response was always the same. "I just feel like God is telling me that we need to do something for him."

The photo of him on the refrigerator held the most prominent spot right next to the handle. Every time Nita got something out of the fridge, his plight and story overpowered her. It started to take on a life all its own, and I was struggling just getting a handle on it myself.

"WE?" I protested. "Are you thinking we should send him a check, support him somehow?"

That was always my go-to, cure all. Keep an arms length distance between my life and theirs, be involved but keep the balance status quo—happy to donate my proceeds, just reluctant, like most people, to surrender my *person*.

Her look was an indictment. It was obvious that my charitable response fell woefully inadequate. She was getting lost in a battle I couldn't engage in—or hadn't engaged in.

Like late-summer thunderclouds, something had to break between a wife with a heart for a boy in Uganda and a husband still pining for the American Dream. My plan after getting married at age 18 was to have kids and work a mortgage and a nest egg. After a difficult bout with infertility getting the firstborn, we had a son. Five years later, right when Nita took her board certification tests, we popped out a girl. By age 30, my decision was to be done with populating my address and be spry enough when the kids were young adults. A weekend visit to the urologist and badda-bing, coast into comfort and mortgage-free bliss. That was the plan, that was the process. That was our life.

Or so I thought.

Finally, we agreed to investigate some options, poke around, do some "what ifs." They ranged from setting up a trust fund in Uganda for William's schooling and housing, to bringing him to America for high school. By this time, I was beginning to break down my defenses of my pre-determined process. But any degree of control was quickly being overrun by unknown prayers of a boy nine thousand miles away.

We looked up a good friend of ours who had emigrated from Kenya. He came to our college town on a student visa, married a body-building teammate, gained citizenship and started a mortgage company. Over lunch, he explained the simple process of bringing a person from another country over on a student visa. It sounded like a no-brainer, and for a moment, there seemed to be some light at the end of this dim tunnel we'd been navigating.

Armed with the name of a local immigration attorney, we set up an appointment, wrote the first of what would become a thousand checks, and blindly walked onto the stage of the biggest play of our lives.

This bit of encouraging information proved to be the blind, pivotal decision and committed us to going on this journey. We both agree now that this was the step where we bit off more than we could chew, and for the next unforeseen future, would chew like crazy. We chewed through expenses beyond our estimations and chewed way past what we thought we could ever endure.

It had been nearly a year since the promise was made from the "I'm so sorry" song. Included in part of the original group who went over to Uganda was a family from Southern California who felt strongly that God was telling them to move there.

Brian and Angela, along with their three teenage children, sold all they had and boarded a plane with no return date. None of them had ever been out of the country before, but by now they had set up a home with two apartments to rent and had been there long enough to establish a handful of reliable contacts. They got us in touch with the resident head pastor of Jireh and got us information from some local ties and a few other Muzungu missionaries about our ideas.

We made contact with those leads, prayerfully felt like we should continue this quest and felt confident the process was ordained and favored. The couple even got us in touch with the name of a "Christian" attorney. Via Western Union, we sent a retainer to this trusted Ugandan lawyer in the amount of one-million shillings—about four-hundred U.S. dollars. This was to get the process of a student visa started, to gain an official birth certificate and get a passport issued. "Plan a trip over, and all will be taken care of by the time you arrive," he told us.

A couple of clicks on Travelocity's web site and Nita's promise had two boarding passes for a trip in the early fall of 2012, that was only a handful of weeks away.

While waiting for the early September departure, other details needed doing. Nita was nesting around the house like she did during her pregnancies. She began to reconfigure our daughter's old bedroom to a more masculine motif—new bedspread, sheets, some shelves and a desk for homework. The closet was emptied of girlie items and replaced with a couple of Nike hoodies, various sports polo shirts, brightly colored shorts and a few pair of "swoosh" branded shoes. There was even a warm winter coat hanging on the back of the door because when William arrived, autumn would be shifting to winter.

Being a guy, I only needed a week's worth of underwear, a few pair of shorts and travel pants in a shoulder pack. But the one thing I did have to prepare for was refrigeration. I'm a type 1 diabetic. Insulin needs to be cool. The weather on the equator is hot and the power grid erratic. I found some of those chemical icepacks at R.E.I. sports store, the kind you smack with your hand and they stay cool for hours. I bought a case. That should do the trick for the two weeks we were going to be there.

The stirrings and preparations were contagious as the story and plans were shared with neighbors, friends and church members who were all living vicariously through the process. The crowd of followers and social media fans were cheering us on as we pushed doors open and prayed. The collective momentum seemed to be lining up like stars, or possibly, an eclipse.

In what seemed like parental déjà vu, we had to once again orchestrate schooling, commuting and functioning through our work schedules to accommodate an arriving young teen in our lives. We found that middle schools to enroll William were limited. They needed to have a special foreign student designation which would allow a nonimmigrant person to come study in America.

Registering for this specific "F-1" was another mound of inking out paperwork. It required a home study by a state certified case worker, and of course, more money.

We finally ended up back at the private Christian school where both our own children went. They gave us a pastor discount and contact info to a few families who had reportedly started with F-1 visas but were now into the adoption process. We kept telling people we weren't on that page.

I mean we weren't imagining the kid sharing our last name, just meatloaf Mondays for a while and some hot shower water for a few semesters.

The September 3 departure date arrived. Nita had carefully sectioned out a portion in her baggage for some new clothes for William—a red-white-and blue American track warm-up that he was to wear in celebration for the jet ride home.

Armed with a slim notebook of required papers and visa receipts we double checked all of our bases. We made the final contact with the Ugandan lawyer who was working on our retainer. He assured us in tones of triumph that "everything was ready for you to come and pick up your boy. You come now," he said.

The local pastor affirmed that he had spoken to the attorney and all looked good. He had made signs for the men's conference I was to teach at his church. He assured us that we would have extra time because the visa and passport processes would be so speedy.

Before we knew it, our well-traveled son, Garrett, and his girlfriend, Bethany, were driving us north two hours to Portland International Airport. The trip allowed us time to reminisce about other jaunts out of country, fond victories of mission trips we have made as a family. Garrett said this one seemed a bit different, bigger, deeper, less to his understanding how it all was going to play out.

I couldn't disagree. As the highway lines zipped past our black Beemer, the more I thought about how this kid in Uganda doesn't look like us, talk like us, or belong to us. Behind the excitement, our journey started to scare the hell out of me.

The flight left just after lunch. I ordered a burger—"please, with everything, and bacon." God knows what I'm going to be eating in Africa. We parted ways with hugs from Garrett and Bethany, slipped through security un-stripped, hallelujah.

We stopped just before boarding to take a quick 'going-to-get William' selfie but the camera failed to click. Realizing immediately I forgot to put in the memory card, I sprinted down to the kiosk and bought the only one they had, a 32 gig super-size.

I remember chuckling that it would hold like 2500 images. I've never taken that many photos even when I was a working photojournalist on a single assignment. I mean how big is this story going to get?

We strapped into Row 37 and settled in to the 28-plus hours of travel ahead of us. The image of William on the refrigerator seemed to becoming into the final tray, the one where the image becomes permanently fixed on the paper.

We were believing that this was the final phase, the last dip in the process. Instead, we were only in the first—and there were more than two trays to follow.

6

PRIORITIES AND SACRIFICES

Sitting in a plane for an extended period gives you the opportunity to reflect on where you're headed.

Surrounded by white noise of jet engines in the utter darkness over the Sahara Desert I pinched myself. I'm going to Africa with my wife, to get a kid I've never met. At what point I thought, did this become a priority? I determined it must have had something to do with that prayer uttered in the shower some months ago, and about a car I fell in love when I was nine years old. It was life priority for sure. The two were connected.

The car was a fast, loud, growling beast of a convertible stuffed with a Ford V-8 motor. It had only two seats—one for the driver, and one for whoever was going to scream. I swore I'd unearth one of those someday, build it to perfection, and never sell it.

For years I scoured car shows and want-ads. I cold-called the select owners of the beast and asked if they knew of any hidden in old barns or mothballs forgotten about. Once I was even told, "It's not for sale" at the end of a shot gun. But the moment I finally found my dream and was winching it onto a car trailer was the exact moment my wife called me from a medical mission trip she was on in Romania. She was in the gothic trenches doing the same kind of dental work in some of the darkest orphanages imaginable that she had done with William.

"What are you doing?" she asked innocently.

"Ummm." I stalled. Guilty and caught.

"I'd rather not say."

"You found a Tiger, didn't you?"

Funny how the wife knows exactly what the mice are doing when the cats away.

"Yes, honey, yes I did, but you remember I sold my other restored car and that's how I got the money." First the money-not-from-the-family cookie-jar line, followed by the I-won't-steal-from-the-cookie-jar-again line.

I rationalized I would fix it, as I had spare money. It sounded so juvenile, like I was trying to make a case for a kid getting a dog.

Ignoring my out-of-whack priorities from her familiar perspective, she steered the conversation back to the mission field and needy kids. I could hear those familiar heart strings of hers being plucked by plight and pity. Once again though, it all wound down to rational practicality. It's impossible to bring one home.

Nita came back from Romania, empty-handed again, and for the next ten years or so we focused ourselves on raising our own kids and not saving the world. We immersed ourselves in church outreaches, and embarked on various mission trips anytime we had opportunity, thus satisfying the need to serve and avoiding the burden to rescue. In between all of that, I built the sweetest, fastest, shiniest, speed-yellow, 1965 Sunbeam Tiger on the West Coast.

There's just half of these cars left from the limited production of 3400 units. As my son and daughter were wrapping up college the last minor detail left to totally complete my life-long car dream was two-seat interior. I had been patiently driving the car for the past few years with beach towels thrown over them. The kids had only a few months of college left, then some of that 'extra money' would shift from the priority of college and be coming my way in the form of leather and padding.

About the same time I was staring just ahead to my 50th birthday. I was starting to work on fine tuning some spiritual nuts and bolts, eternal kind of priorities, what I would leave, rather than what I was assembling. Things like my legacy. Like sacrifice. *What could I lay of value on the altar of God that would drive me to the next level?* I even prayed that altar request—aloud from the shower one morning. Before I could utter the closing amen, I'm certain I heard an excited voice from somewhere above bounce off my shower walls.

Something like, "Glad you asked! I know just the thing for the altar." To which God seemed to be reminding me again now, on our way to Africa.

Endless hours of restless travel, and a couple of glasses of airline white wine and my bride was pretty much ready for the wheelbarrow to bed. Yet, at the midnight landing in Entebbe, Uganda, through the layer of smoky blackness from burning trash, she was race-ready and energized.

Our luggage came off the belt earlier than the rest, and before I could blink out the sleepy dust or the irritation from the African atmosphere, she had her baggage cart loaded and was zipping for the exit.

I expected her excitement. What I didn't expect was what she was so excited about. Blasting past the signs with various tourist names on them she spied the leather safari hat that was the identifying mark of the pastor from Jireh. Closing the gap between them was William, scooting across the floor with ragged, holey shoes three-sizes too big, waving wildly with one hand while his other hand clutched his pants, which were about two sizes too large.

"Oh, my God," she squealed, "there he is!!!" Instantly she abandoned the goods on the cart, which crashed into mine, and was immediately engulfed in a full-on swirling hug from a very happy, bald-shaven young black boy with the widest white smile I had ever seen. He presented her with a bouquet of droopy roadside flowers, which were now squished nearly beyond recognition from his having been holding them for hours in baited expectation.

"You came back!" he said, wiping away a tear of joy in a muffled voice from behind Nita's arms. "I knew you would come back, I just knew it."

My introduction to William was a hug with one arm and the other outstretched recording video. I'm a freelance advertising photographer by trade and always have a camera at the ready. I captured some great moments with his little face on input overload.

The forty-kilometer drive to the heart of Kampala was sketchy at best, with four of us plus two extra children about the same age as William crammed into a pickup cab. Parental questions were rising up in my protective nature. Why are these kids out at this time of night?

We stopped about halfway there, in the middle of the two-lane road, surrounded by a frenzy of people crisscrossing the roadway to the deafening beat of bass music. Those two guest kids suddenly opened the door and piled out into oncoming traffic.

"Make sure you watch the bags!" the pastor warned as he swiftly got out of the pick-up truck to escort the parentless adolescents to somewhere. His voice was loud enough to carry over to the thug-looking characters milling about at the edge of the road. The truck was resting high-centered on the curb median in the dark, barely lit by passing cars, right out in the open with the keys in the pastor's pocket. "Helpless Americans: come steal our stuff and mug us in the process."

He disappeared across the road and down a dirt alleyway chasing the kids. *This doesn't look good,* I thought. So I got out of the truck and stood, leaning right next to the cab window where Nita was sitting in some sort of protective posture. The chaos and booming bass tones of the music was enough to put me on high-alert. I scanned the surroundings with the intensity of a wannabe covert Army ranger. Of course, being the only white guy within miles, I was like a beacon in the middle of the road, in the middle of the night, which drew all kinds of immediate and surreptitious attention. It was a tense 15 or 20 minutes we waited for the pastor to finally return. This was a huge first step even out of my world-traveler comfort zone.

Around 2 a.m., after being bumped and beaten by the potholes, we made an unmarked turn off the main drag behind another disco inferno. We stopped inches from a large set of steel doors guarding the entrance to a pitch black compound surrounded by razor wire. Across the fortified barrier were the hand-painted words, "guest house, you are welcome."

The horn blared—twice—loud enough to wake the entire neighborhood. A young African man, lit only by our headlights right in his face, unbolted the door and squeaked them open enough for us to drive through.

The door man guided us to a steel room door with a large padlock, swept the wall with his hand, and flicked on a compact fluorescent light which hung from a single wire in the middle of a plaster ceiling.

"You are welcome." he said, dumping the bags onto the floor in the corner.

Under my breath, I murmured, "I…um, I haven't said thank you yet." There was a little barrier in the communication.

"We've a big day tomorrow. We'll go and see the lawyer to get William's paperwork in order," the pastor said with confidence. "Let's get an early start, get all of this finished and so we can do the men's conference at my church."

Seemed like it was all routine. Just like home. You have trusted contacts, goals for the day, stuff gets done, William goes to America. I like a man who works a plan. But there was this thing hanging around…T.I.A.

"William will stay with me. You must not stay in the same room with the boy, otherwise people in this country will look upon you as child traffickers or worse," he warned. "William and I shall be good 'till the morning. Make sure you lock this entry. It's safer that way."

Safer than what? I thought.

Looking at Nita's face as she scanned the room, I could see the rapid departure of new arrival syndrome wearing off. The bare-faced details of our new surroundings were rapidly setting in. Putting my hand up in between her face and mine, I made the first of many sacrificial jokes.

"I don't want to hear how bad this pig hole of a room is," I righteously stated. "This journey is going to be one of many more sacrifices. We both are going to have to buck up to get through the next couple of weeks."

She nodded. And then she looked to the bed. The double bed had only one, single-sized sheet.

"So I guess the first thing to decide is, do we try and sleep both of us on the only sheet? Or do we try to use it as a cover and take the risk of what ever is going to join us from that bugs nest of a mattress?" she said.

My last ounce of husband "fix-it" kicked in and just before a total jet-lag shut-down. I reached for my stuff sack sleeping bag liner clipped to my carry on pack. The one I always carry to foreign destinations just in case I find myself in critter challenged sleeping quarters with missing linens, or even in some cases, missing beds.

We joked a bit more about the facilities, but just around the footboard of the bed in the "wet bathroom" behind the wall lay in waiting the next morning's challenges. I hadn't recognized anything in there resembling a shower head, just a hand operated sink spigot that also doubled as a bidet.

We unzipped the slender stuff sack covering and threw it under the mosquito netting which we quickly pulled behind us. The light blue quilted nylon floated over us. Well, most of us. It was like covering up with a dog blanket. I laid awake for a few more moments but Nita passed out nearly instantly.

In those moments that first night in the darkness and unfamiliarity, I reminisced about that yellow car of my dreams. The same one I saw get wrapped up in cellophane, and loaded onto a super car truck transport to California. The same rare car God asked me to sell a month before we arrived, that rumbled its way out of my life forever. It had been laid on an altar, for some reason to get me here.

I felt paid up in my part of the sacrifices. But it was just the beginning. For both of us.

7

FAREWELLS AND SQUAWKING GIFTS

My watch alarm went off at sunrise.

Nita was already up and operating the drippy water spigot, aka shower, behind the wall in the wet bathroom.

What I mean by "operating" the water spigot, I mean that when I looked around the corner the scene had the strange resemblance to pole dancing. She was laughing hysterically and certainly didn't have enough water to even finish the job. So I set out to find her some sort of tub or pail to augment the water shortage. And with a wide smile on my face, left a few dollar bills on the sink for a tip.

Throwing on some short pants and flip flops, I unbolted the steel door and ventured out shirtless into the smoky morning.

I heard some splashing. It sounded like someone doing laundry. It echoed inside the 10 foot walls of the Pacify Guest House, all of which was surrounded with juvenile art, murals of cows, giraffes and pasture scenes, and topped with razor wire coils. Rounding the corner of the dungeon-like corridor, I find dutiful William, in the same clothes as the night before. He's washing the vehicle with the bald tires of its red clay, with a muddy, ragged, brown cloth about the size of a napkin. One hand was skillfully splashing the water up from a yellow pail, while the rag was wiping and using gravity to rinse the chocolate from the cars body panels.

"Very nice." I said, walking around the vehicle inspecting the work. "You did all of this with just that much water?"

There was maybe a couple of liters in that small pale and though this was no detail shop, he certainly impressed me with doing so much with so little.

"I got up early to wash the truck so we could go into town clean and get what we needed to do," he said, barely looking up from the work.

"Well, you are doing a great job young man," I said. "Just wait till you get to America, we have hoses that spray water all over the car."

The look on his face was that standard look you get with any world travel experience. If a local doesn't quite understand you, they smile and nod. Conversely, if we don't quite understand them, typical Americans will smile, nod and talk louder. I wasn't finding a lot to talk about right away and it was certainly too early to talk louder. But I was so struck with his servant-like character that it set me back a bit. What I didn't realize was how much serious deprogramming and reprogramming was in our future with blending our vast cultural differences. I mean, just the realization that a young teen would get up before sunrise to wash a car was about as unusual as a Muzungu coming out of the sleeping room without a shirt on. So I found out.

The lawyer's office on the fourth floor of E-tower, was a fairly new building in the heart of Kampala. Home and work to nine million souls, fifty-thousand boda-boda motor-scooter taxis, two-thousand diesel-belching 14-passenger transport vans and a gazillion autos, all honking their horns and going no where fast.

We walked a few blocks to E-tower from a church parking lot where we got a great daily parking rate. Arriving at the tiled, open-air entry, the first thing I noticed were the uneven steps. First a small rise, then a big, followed by a few others of varying heights. So naturally I'm thinking, rather than break a front tooth on this stair trap, let's take the elevator, only to discover that was the first thing that wasn't going to work today. It wasn't near finished. In fact, it was barely started. There were two gaping, open doorways at the corner of the building with not even a stripe of yellow warning tape across them. Somebody could have inadvertently fallen to their death.

"TIA," I sighed.

And so up the uneven steps, eight flights to the Christian attorney we had hired, a guy named Steve.

Behind the hollow-core door, the office was portioned in half with cheap wood paneling attached to wobbly frames and another set of hollow doors. A few feet of space, just enough for the door to swing in and for a receptionist with a laptop to be parked in line with a wooden bench for two. There was one stray office chair, in the expansive waiting room barely an arms length wide.

"This guy is a real professional," the pastor said, taking off his leather signature safari hat. "This will all be good in a few days."

We entered into his tiny office and did what I call the "big sit." Small talk and cordialities, smiles, handshakes and assurances that all of the legal work was in progress.

"It will all be certainly completed in just a few days," Steve told us through a wide gap in his Chiclet gum smile. He adjusted his Yoko Ono half-glasses and opened a file that I assumed was ours. He shuffled it around his desk of other scattered papers and pulled out a single sheet. According to him, it was an official passport visa request he said he filed, but thinking back, I never really confirmed a name on the paper, or the folder either.

"Oh yes, this is Tuesday and by a week from Wednesday next at the latest, all will be good. You come back then and see me."

He waved his hand confidently and tucked the official paper back into the skinny file burying it under the desk mess. "Go to Masaka, teach at this pastor's church, say your goodbyes and return on Monday. All will be done and you can have a restful time in Uganda."

After standing and thanking him, the pastor stopped us in our departure tracks.

"I believe God wants us to pray over these proceedings and this process."

The lawyer chimed in with his enthusiastic approval, saying he always prayed like this with his clients.

Right after the final word the two locals proclaimed, "Ameena," which we repeated. It means "amen," which is to say, "may it be as we all have spoken."

On the secure words of the lawyer we left the city. All of the details we believed were being signed and stamped in wizard-like fashion by his assistants and secretary, behind the cloak of money we paid him. Four hundred American dollars is about one-million Ugandan schillings. It sounded like enough to move mountains, and yet, all we needed was a birth certificate and a passport, and an exit visa stamp in said passport. He gave us his word.

William's mother, Regina, we had heard, was running a small produce shop again while living in a squatter area of inner Kampala. The pastor had found a phone number and made contact a few weeks before our arrival. She wanted to host us for a meal. This is a typical gesture of respect and trust; what's more, her offering and preparation were clearly way over the top from what she could afford. But she suggested that it was a must to visit her as a way to honor her sacrifice. Never mind that she hadn't seen William for more than a year.

We were excited to meet her, both to pay our respects mother-to-mother, family-to-family, and to bring her a few gifts. Nita had gotten a beautiful silver cross necklace and assembled some photos of our family in a nice frame she could either stand up or hang. Beyond that, a woman in our church had crocheted a wonderful green and black blanket with our Three Sixteen mission statement words in bold print, "Love. Give. Have."

Three Sixteen was a church Nita and I and a fellow Razorwire Ministries prison pastor started a little over a year ago in addition to our day jobs. Initially, it was going to be a safe place for inmates to land when they got out of the Salem correctional institution prison ministry. We were developing into a congregation of about 50, rock 'n' roll worshipers, raw-life Christians who I challenged weekly to move boldly into each one's God-sized calling, like going to Africa to see your gifts outside the walls of a church.

The gifts we were giving the mother felt like the perfect set of sentiments of respect. After all, she was about to transfer and trust her parental rights to her son to total strangers.

Her shack wasn't that far from the semi-opulence of E-tower. But economically, it was as far as it could be. It was lost in a sea of temporary sheds selling fish, vegetables, and old ship cargo containers brightly painted yellow and red selling mobile phone time. Women walking with those classic African parcels on their heads, the scent of burnt tires, and mounds of compost at the dirt street corners wasn't powerful enough to overtake the other smells of urine, and diesel.

In a sea of brown, we stood out. Nearly every single African soul noticed and stared at us, obviously displaced and out of context in an unfamiliar urban jungle.

"Turn here," William said. The neighborhood was all coming back to him—the faded memories of landmarks, broken trees still snagged on power lines, the way trash was piled at strategic street corners. "Yes this is the way, it's down this path between the other buildings."

There was a trail through what looked like a city dump in a low lying area of a dry flood bed. Shanty lean-to buildings with store merchants in them dotted randomly. A few structures with skimmed brick and small porches were near the main path, one with a child, naked, standing just outside the front door, pouring cups of water over his head, shivering, and rubbing his wiggling body clean.

"Stay here with the windows rolled up and stay in the car until I get back," the pastor said as he parked the car as far as the debris would allow us to drive. He gave us that danger stare just like he did the first night along the roadway. "I will be right back when I make contact with her."

He locked the doors, and quickly leapt into the trash-line trail, bounding his way toward a small corridor between two mud huts. No more than the moment he disappeared, is when it felt like a beacon light got switched onto the car. Kids on ratty bicycles stopped and started waving, pointing and shouting "Muzungu! Muzungu!."

This made us nervously wave and draw even more unnecessary attention to ourselves. Men started coming out of seams in between boarded plank walls and out from around abandoned vehicles, staring, assessing. For a few moments it felt like all the laser gazes were closing in from all sides, and step by step, black curiosity seekers were beginning to surround the car.

The mid-afternoon sun was cooking on high, raising the temperature and the stress. Sweat was beginning to run down my spine. Our conversations muted to humming. It had been twenty minutes. Then suddenly, like a loud bang in a horror movie, someone pounded on the rear glass. It was the pastor.

"We can go now," he said waving his hand hurriedly. "But we must go quickly."

I'm thinking, does quickly mean to hurry up and try to out run the mob? It didn't matter. We ejected outa' the car like a fighter pilot without hydraulic controls, because in this environment, we didn't have any.

The maze led us over mud puddles, more debris, around roaming chickens, and back to where two of William's young step brothers were playing uncomfortably close to the small fire. This was the mom's kitchen, where lunch was cooking.

Regina greeted us with a wide smile, animated happiness and multiple hugs. The pastor interpreted from her how much of an honor it was to meet us. Repeatedly, she seemed overly thankful for what we were about to do for William.

She was young and slender, taller than I expected, and beautiful. Her skin was like butter chocolate with a glowing sheen. Her bashfulness and emotion was like that of a girl greeting her favorite guests at a sweet-sixteen party.

She had just given birth month or so ago, and as we ducked into the doorway to sit down, someone placed the baby in Nita's arms. The two moms did the cooing thing, seeming to speak the same language. Nita tried to ask the name of the new little girl, but there was too much crowd confusion from all of us trying to squeeze into the shanty..

"Her name from now on is to be Nita," the pastor said as William's mother kept repeating the name of my wife. As Nita was seated, Regina knelt below my wife, patting her knee like she was bowing to a queen. Her gratefulness and praise was overflowing.

Outside the doorway, contrasted by the inky darkness of the interior, friends and other mothers were busily getting the plates of food ready. It seemed like a good time for the gifts we brought so Nita handed off the baby to William. It was his first time he'd ever seen or known he had a stepsister. Initial awkwardness aside, he went right with the flow and began swaying the child as she lay across his knees.

As each gift was presented, Regina wailed and raised her hands in praises to God. She would then talk so fast I don't think the pastor had enough time to translate all that was said. But as the old saying goes, what was played out in those moments, actions were speaking louder than words.

She prepared and served a grand meal. In fact, the pastor mentioned that this may have cost her nearly a month's wages. My heart was heavy and humbled at the same time. Looking around what she had versus what she gave is a moment of shame I hope I never forget.

Almost silently and unnoticed, a man slipped into the doorway and sat in the nearest darkest corner. It was William's step dad. I'm sure I was introduced to him but I never caught his name. My only thoughts, as I tried my best to be civil, was that this was the man who, by his Muslim faith, chose to *not* bring William into the family when the boy's mother married him. I couldn't help picturing a pre-school aged boy, fatherless by what was believed to be an unfortunate accident, and then again, fatherless by rejection and religion.

After lunch and gifts, we took pictures like we were at a family reunion. Regina walked us out of the maze and introduced us to nearly everyone we passed by in the overcrowded slum. She seemed proud and now of some status to the locals of being in the company of a white couple and also hitting the lotto of giving away her first born, bound to America.

As we got back near the car, there stood a slightly elevated hut made with scraps of pallet wood and found material that could take a nail and stay affixed. It reminded me of the forts I made as a kid with junk from house construction sites.

A hand-painted sign was nailed to the corner with her last name on it. Separated by an oversized comma was another word next to hers which translated, "proprietor." Regina's shop had just a handful of items inside, a couple of pieces of fly-ridden fruit, a tube of toothpaste, and a roll of toilet paper. A cobbled-together wooden box served as the counter. One of William's step brothers was minding the till. He was seated on the floor, hanging one leg out of the opening to the fort.

The two were so unfamiliar with each other that it was more than awkward. It confirmed again William being the lone outsider to a family that moved on with out him.

What seemed nagging and odd was the way William and Regina related to each other. They seemed to have a relationship but at the same time, not. There was the apparent love from the blood connection, the occasional hug, and lots of laughter between them. But as with most remarried African families with children from a previous fathers, William didn't really know her as a mother. He was being sent away so young there wasn't that bond. It was almost as if he was just another face in the midst of casual strangers.

This was the first family good-bye on our checklist of contacts before William left to be educated elsewhere. It seems everyone is a cousin and connected in some way. The pastor stopped off at a cousin's church, where I preached at a prayer revival while three women openly breast fed their children in the front row. The distraction was so great I hardly remember what my subject was.

The pastor also has some cousins, David and Merianne, who ran a children's day school on the outer highway ring a short jaunt north of Kampala. He said "it's not far" out of our way. That expression would later become the sister comment to, "it's no problem." Which basically meant, it's going to take forever, it's a long way out of our way, and "no problem" means it's entirely my problem.

David and Merianne were a late-twenties couple, both college educated and entrepreneurs who were just getting their legs under them running a children's day school. Like any start-up, they were filling a great need but also were trying to become self-reliant and in charge of their own destiny.

Their problems of corruption and deception were all too familiar in Uganda. Their landlord, whom they were renting a high-walled compound from, was seeing their apparent success and trying to gouge them by successively raising rent. They were honest people, but the vicious circle of kids in need who couldn't pay kept the ends moving faster than they could meet.

With nearly every other breath they praised "the God who provides" and said that "perseverance will bring everything into success in God's timing." Certainly words I've heard and said from the pulpit a hundred times, but was now seeing a couple really live it out.

We noticed during the tour of the facility that the kids on sleeping mats didn't have blankets. We were instantly stirred to help. So once we got into Masaka, one of the first things we did was negotiate with a shop keeper a bulk price on a bunch of blankets. We used some of the money our church gave us for charitable work. Those funds bought a dozen colorfully soft blankets and we planned to give them when we'd be back through following week.

The couple who came over on Nita's first trip, Brian and Angela, were now living in Masaka and had rented a great home from a local pastor. It had two small apartments where were stayed the week of waiting for the big-city lawyer to work with the visa office.

Brian and Angela had a three-year old Ugandan boy at their home. A number of Sundays ago they were asked to hold him before he died.

Story goes, he was born to a 16 year-old mother out of wedlock—some say she was raped—and then left abandoned in the mother's front yard to die at eighteen months. He had suffered multiple lacerations, a deep gouge over his right eye, he was burned in a few places, and he had a broken leg. They were asked to hold him so it may give him some final comfort. He was now thriving in their care.

Brian looks astonishingly like every image of Jesus in print. Long beard, peaceful smile. His wife, Angela, is an effervescent bottle blond with a southern drawl. They were so moved by the little boys circumstance, they vowed this might just have been their calling to come to Uganda. They named him Joseph "Jo Jo" Freedom and committed to make him their own, however long it took.

Their sentiment and commitment I admired but didn't want that much on our plate with William. Stick to the plan, he's a student, not a son.

Our bags hit the bare concrete floor in the two-room apartment. We gave one room to William and we took the other. Both had twin beds, arrgh!

We unpacked some clothes brought over for William to wear while we were there, and also laid aside the ones to travel home in. Jeans, Nike shirts, a white hoodie sweatshirt for going to church in the following day, Sunday, for the big blessing and dancing send-off.

The Sunday service was nearly three hours long. After the first two hours had passed the first worship team was soaked through with sweat. No one in Uganda is on time so the service "officially gets underway', when all the late-comers eventually get there.

William's leaving and going with the American family started a procession of speakers and prayers. Nita spoke about how they met and what William did to her heart. I spoke and prayed over him and the "family" he was leaving that had suddenly emerged from the banana fields all adorned in colorful dresses and pageantry.

After church we piled into the trusty Toyota HiLux truck and headed west to a village to see William's grandfather for the last time.

"It's not far," said the pastor after we had been on the highway to Rwanda for nearly an hour. We turned off the paved road and later took an abrupt right turn over a ditch and into a banana field.

"Is this a trail or a road?" I asked. The initial bounce off the road about pitched me out of the front passenger window. Green leaves from a Gilligan's Island re-run were wiping both sides of the truck. We were zipping through the agriculture like we were being chased by the fruit police.

We came to the end of a row and right into an area where about twenty more relatives were seated outside the grandparent's home.

"How in the heck did you ever find this place?" I asked the pastor.

"Oh, I have been here before," he said so matter of fact.

"Perrrfect," I muttered. "We're never going to find our way out, and no one is ever going to know where we are." Checked my mobile phone, not even a single bar.

A tall, elderly and sure-footed, African man in a long white tunic, with a robust smell of gin, greeted me at the truck door, and with some of the longest fingers I had ever seen, and shook Nita's and my hand. He then took our hands guiding them to the line of women and men relatives and we went down the line. Lots of smiling and nodding. Supposedly all distant relatives, so far removed that taking care of him apparently wasn't anyone's direct responsibility.

Scorching hot tea was poured, more introductions, some explanations of photos on the wall, the big sit was in full swing. There were so many people crammed into the mud and leaf hut and hanging through the exterior windows that I couldn't even fit them all into a wide-angle photo.

The grandparents had gifts, which caught us both off guard. I felt a bit awkward like showing up at a Christmas gift exchange without my part, but they insisted it was just a gesture to send blessings with William before he departed.

Wrapped in banana leaves. I suspected was an avocado. Now before you scratch your head thinking it's such a small token, these avo's grow to the size of a bowling balls. I'm not sure what the significance of the tasty green guacamole fruit was, but we thanked then enthusiastically none the less.

The next banana wrapped gift was moving a little bit. When we both went to grab it and pose for quick picture. It squawked, like a live chicken. Because it was a chicken.

"They give you the chicken because as a sign of prosperity that you will not be in need," said the pastor over the humorous cheers of the relatives.

We thanked them again and posed for a few more pictures. William poked fun with his grandfather and laughed nearly the whole time we were there. I asked him how close he remained to this man since he went to the orphanage, and he said he'd only seen him a couple of times.

The trip back out of the banana field wasn't exactly the same way in. I felt more lost than ever, like I wanted to send up a signal flare to find my way.

"Oh, here is the road." the pastor said as we pulled out of the grandparent's clearing and onto what he called, the road. It wasn't any more marked out than the one we came in, but if you say potato, I say cow trail. Same thing.

On the ride back, the auntie whom William stayed with on occasion told us she wanted us to give her annual plane tickets to America to check up on how her nephew was doing. As politely as we could muster, we told her how difficult that would be, but as always, something gets lost in translation and perception. I found myself annoyed. William was orphaned for nearly seven years, and all of the sudden when his circumstances are about to change, hordes of shirt-tail relatives appear out of nowhere demanding their piece of some golden pie.

Forgive me for my insensitivity. We were not taking on any excess baggage.

8

PLAN B

For the next few days, William was with Nita doing exploring the local town and doing some tourist shopping. The plan was to do the men's conference Monday and Tuesday, then return to Kampala, where in our minds, a quick couple of papers to sign and a few days in the city would have us catching a flight home late that week.

Ugandans are never on time; same day maybe, on time, never. So that's what my first day's topics tried to address. Integrity, I said starts by being on time.

Ironically, the second day drew even more men to the conference, one of which was a Kenyan named Edward. He arrived smartly dressed and was an acquaintance of Brian and Angela. Actually, he was their garbage man. Edward was also part time pastor, or a local pastor and part time garbage man, depending on the day.

The days teaching that Edward really got excited about is what I call "The Two Pillars." Translated in Ugandan, "Two Impegees." They are: "Speak the truth, even if the truth leads to your death. And, Do what you say, even if doing what you say ruins your reputation." A take from Deuteronomy 23:23.

Edward came up to me at the day's end saying those two concepts of character were going to change his life forever. Admittedly, he said there where were decisions he was putting off changing but thanks to the Pillar teachings, he vowed to be undeniably more honest. Other men said the same. Edward and I become fast friends. He blessed and prayed for William, Nita and I, and we pledged to stay in touch.

Which brings me back to Steve the lawyer.

We were calling Steve to check up on the progress of William's paperwork every day. We were trying to settle a nagging uneasiness in our guts. He wasn't returning our calls. Our nerves were just beginning to fray.

Lawyer Steve, according to his secretary, was constantly "unavailable,." First, it was a family issue, then something personal. He was in court, then on vacation. The pit of my stomach began to burn, and it wasn't from bland mash posho or the beans we had for nearly every meal.

The pastor kept making positive sounding assurances but it began to sound as hollow as the promises our Christian lawyer's office had been making. Nita and I still had enough time, we thought, to make everything work out. It's who we are: get-it-done people, even in the face of adversity. Even on foreign soil.

Even with our heightened concern, the pack-up plan to go to Kampala stayed in motion. The day after the men's conference we drove up the mountain to Jireh to get the metal box of all William's worldly goods and to say farewell to the kids, staff and his friend, Paul.

When William got his vision, Paul was one of the kids he confided in. Like other kids, Paul didn't think the vision was even possible. But when a rumor came to Jireh that two boys would be going to America, a miscommunication from a couple that was looking at Paul, he stepped up his prayer game. After more research, it was discovered that Paul was too old to be eligible for a student visa. That day, the two of them held hands, walked out the gate together, and parted company. Paul to stay in Uganda, William to fly to America.

The scratched-up, blue-painted, metal foot-locker contained the English Bible Nita has sent him months before, a few worn-down pencils, some note book pads, an old school uniform, green shirt, shorts and a belt. There were bits of soap, lotion and a loose double-sided straight razor. It was the kind my grandfather used to clamp down into his pearl-handled shaver.

"What is this for?" I asked William.

"Oh, that is for trimming my nails," he said like it was no big deal. "They give those to all the kids."

William pawed through the contents and gave away everything in his box, reluctantly, even the Bible we had sent over to him.

"It can be replaced when we get home, kids need it more here." Nita told him.

We went back for the final pack-up at Brian and Angela's. They gave us a blessing to send us off, and we prayed that getting their JoJo back to America would go as smooth and what this all appeared to be.

Angela did a couple of those great southern "hoo-ya's" and dished out a handful of the warmest grits and gravy-biscuit hugs I've ever been served. Their little boy—"Jo-Row" I affectionately called him—was fat-lipped sad to see us go too.

"I promise I will see you again my little friend," I knelt down and told him. Then heard that voice inside me say, "ya, gotta' quit doing that."

We had squeezed out all the events we could and left back for Kampala. Time was becoming a commodity we couldn't afford to trade away for the rest of this trip. We had a late afternoon appointment with the lawyer, and in order to beat the traffic and not get choked out completely, we had to make good time on the drive. We headed out with the pastor again at the helm, Nita and William in the back and me riding shotgun.

Once we hit the first outer ring of the traffic circle and into the traffic jam we slammed into the city like we hit a brick wall.

"I know a short cut," the pastor said as he cranked the steering across and behind a corner grasshopper stand. He darted around a guy selling chickens and bounced over a gully onto a dirt road. My stress level skyrocketed.

We arrived again at E-tower with about five minutes to spare before our 4:30 p.m. scheduled appointment. Shoot, that's practically a day early in Ugandan time. The elevator shaft was still an inoperable death shaft, the same strand of yellow tape still guarding the opening. Up the stairs to the fourth floor we stampeded.

"Good afternoon sir and madam," the lawyer's secretary said with a hint of insincerity in her voice.

"Where's Mr. Ste—?"

"He got called into late court."

"At nearly five p.m.?"

She smirked.

"He said he would see you first thing tomorrow morning, about 9 a.m." With that, she stood up, like she was ready to catch the last boat off the island or something.

The pastor, always the guy with the tomorrow-will-be-better attitude, expressed his cordialities to the office woman as Nita and I froze, stunned, silent, confused.

Laying on the bed that night again with the single blue cover laired up under the bug netting, we began to allow the fretting concerns to seep out into a myriad of "what-ifs."

Our mutual suspicions were met with logic as we tried to make excuses for the culture. We rationalized the most catastrophic scenarios because so much was going right. But never in our worst scenarios did we imagine where we'd find ourselves the next morning.

We got to E-tower early, just before 8 a.m., trying to catch our lawyer before any trial excuses could materialize. We sat on the floor, in the elevator area just outside his locked office. The clock clicked close to nine and then slipped right on past. At nearly 10 a.m., we heard the slow clopping of heeled shoes coming up the stairs. As a woman's head cleared the last landing and the secretary spotted us, the cadence became even slower, to a weary trod. I think Christian Lawyer Steve's secretary knew she was about to crawl into the lion's den.

Nita always says to never mess with a momma bear. We hadn't even gotten a birth certificate, but already she seemed to be adopting the growling mama role on William's behalf.

"Where's the lawyer?" Nita demanded, standing toe-to-toe with the secretary.

"He's still in court. He will be back later."

"Then we will just sit here and wait for his return."

Nita's eyes didn't leave the woman for nearly two hours. The secretary fumbled about the laptop playing solitaire and trying to ignore the steady piercing.

Lawyer Steve's clerk, who stepped in and out periodically, claimed he had been in contact with the absent attorney. When? Where? What was filed? Who had it? What could we do to get the documents? His sporadic updates nearly always contradicted the secretary's. We began to put the math together. Nothing was adding up.

I was pacing in and out of the office, back and forth from the door to the open elevator shaft with tape across it. I must have looked down that 40-foot hole dozens of times, thinking, picturing revenge of some sort. My stomach growled. Maybe from hunger, more likely from the stress of being out of control.

I headed down two flights of stairs to a small café to get something to eat. Nita said she was staying put.

The café was strategically located right next to the stairs, which made it impossible for the lawyer to make his way to the office without passing it. I ran back up to get

Nita so she could have a break and told her we could burrow our stakeout down at the café table for the rest of the day.

The folks who ran the café were, coincidently, the cousins of the pastor, who after hearing about our plans and plight, gave us the low-down on the missing counselor.

He was notoriously crooked. A womanizer, a thief. Con-artist. Our story seemed to be the one that broke the camel's back. All five of the servers and owners told us they would be on the lookout for slimy Steve and took our mobile phone number for a quick alert.

Additionally, they told us that we could file for a Ugandan passport on William's behalf if only we had a birth certificate in hand. Once we did, they claimed the country's office was only a short distance across town and that securing the document took only took a few days. That sounded encouraging, since a few days is all we had left.

Leaving the last of her chicken and chips behind, Nita marched back up the stairs to catch the secretary just before she left for lunch. Again, she demanded the birth certificate.

"It's locked up in Steve's office," she said, "and I don't have a key."

I wanted to push harder, get in her face a bit.

"But if you are found to be breaking the law or anything that looks like you are trying to go around the system, you will be denied everything," the pastor warned me. "You lose all you've tried."

So in other words, play the waiting game and hope. That approach has never been my way to get things done, but we were in Uganda and I didn't have home-court advantage.

Nita followed the secretary down the two flights of stairs back to the café, grilling her on the whereabouts of the William's birth certificate. They ran into the lawyer's assistant, who, after the secretary left, offered us an option.

In a nutshell, he said we could "hire" him to file the documents. He told us nothing had been done. All of our money was spent, but he thought he could convince Steve to surrender the birth certificate and then run it personally over to the passport office and get a rush put on.

Cost to us? About 300,000 shillings, or $120. He even offered to write us up a contract for his services to ensure some degree of integrity. He wanted half down and half when he delivered the passport.

We'd already been scammed. What looked like a way to dodge another scam seemed to be another scam. But what choices did we have? Facing an immanent departure, we had to set aside our boiling emotions and make some sound decisions.

"At least we will have another person looking for lawyer Steve," I said to Nita. "And being as this assistant runs this kind of stuff through the passport office all the time, maybe he can call in some favors."

Now who was sounding optimistic in the face of failure?

It was a gamble. But we didn't have a Plan B. So we took the clerk up on his offer, paid him half, and watched him run out of E-tower on an urgent mission. We held the table at the cafe as our stakeout. Seated faithfully with us was a 12-year old Ugandan boy, silently looking at us with trusting eyes.

Around dusk, the white-shirted assistant came huffing by the table saying he had found Steve and knew where the birth certificate was. He would have to get with the secretary to locate it first thing in the morning.

Weary, we agreed to meet at 9 a.m. As I laid there a second night listening to Nita grunt out moans of anger during her troubled sleep, I tried to imagine a plan that would save the day.

It was becoming painfully obvious plan A was disintegrating and I needed to stay focused on the task, not the emotions.

My only plan now was to get the goods we paid for, get the papers and passport, and somehow, get the three of us the hell outa' there.

9

THROWIN' A HAIL MARY

The next open door God put in front of us in getting William to America was one I nearly kicked down.

With our scheduled departure at midnight the next day, we were hoping for some kind of eleventh hour miracle that Friday. Every second seemed to tick by faster.

Again we rose early to get whatever jump on the day we could. Nita camped out in Lawyer Steve's office, resuming the third day of her staring down the secretary. She steadily needled the beleaguered secretary about the whereabouts of missing person attorney, and the only promised paper, the birth certificate, we needed to even jump-start a Hail Mary miracle.

The assistant and the secretary were having mobile phone conversations off and on during the morning. Something was brewing. Emotions were getting raw. Nita was hounding the secretary with demands like, "Get that slimy crook on the phone."

Our newly hired double agent, the would-be-do-gooder assistant, checked in every couple of hours with no news of Steve's whereabouts or the location of the birth certificate. In the meantime, he had spoken to his connection at the passport office and he suggested we get William's photos taken, and go to the internet café upstairs to download the passport forms so we could leap into the process once we got the elusive birth document in hand.

Around noon-ish, the assistant came in with some promising news. He had just got off the phone to another of his professional contacts. This one was at the U.S. Embassy Visa office. He handed us a crinkled slip of paper with a name and a phone number scribbled on it saying if we got there within the half hour, during this guy's lunch break we could circumvent some of the red tape for the final visa even before we got the passport.

For a little money, of course.

When you're in a foreign country, playing by their rules, and unsure who you can trust, you have no other options.

I looked over our third-storey balcony, everything in the city had ground to a halt. Even if we were to run the three blocks back to the truck parked in the church lot, we would never make the rendezvous with the Embassy contact across town before his break was over. The only way was for the four of us to get on a couple of boda boda motorcycle taxis and snake our way through the mess. Motorcycles was something Nita avowed she would never do, not for anyone, for any reason. After racing to the ground floor and swinging a leg over the seat, she yelled back to William on the other bike.

"I'm only doing this for you!" she said shaking her finger in his direction.

Sandwiching her between the driver, who slid up to ride on the gas tank, I leap-frogged over the tail light and grabbed the seat rail behind me. Nita's eyes were clamped down water tight.

"Let's do this!" I said to the driver. "You're gonna' wanna' see this!" I yelled over the traffic to Nita, "It'll be like nothing you've ever seen or done before. Bucket list kinda stuff."

With zero language interpretation delays with the drivers, the two abruptly opened up the throttles and dove into first narrow gap in traffic. Somehow they spliced enough room for the both of them between the rear view mirrors, missing our heads and the bumpers rubbing by our knees.

We raced up the ramp to the Embassy security check, quickly got our back packs searched and passed through the metal detector. Under a carport-like cover were some lockers behind another security person and a long wooden bench with a number of locals seated waiting, looking like human cobwebs. It looked like they had been there for days. Unfamiliar with the process we went right to the information window and said we were here to see the man's name whom I attempted to read off the paper.

The guard at the window motioned for me to give him the paper. After reading it he said something to the guy behind who motioned toward the phone. A few moments later the guard put the phone in the cradle and said one word. "No."

"No?" I said. "What do you mean, No! What the heck just happened?"

The guard behind the bullet proof glass yelled under the stainless gulley tray at the pastor. The pastor shrugged. T.I.A. style.

"He said the man is not here today. We should come back on Monday."

"We're not supposed to be here Monday!" I yelled. "Didn't our guy just talk to this guy and say that we were coming?"

"We should just go back and continue to wait for the lawyer," the pastor said with his African C'est la vie.

The defeated look on Nita's face ramped me up to a new level of anger. Before, I was just really disappointed and disillusioned. Now, my war swords were being drawn. Someone was about to be quartered.

On the way back to the office, William and the Pastor disappeared out of view into the motorized meltdown. They went off the authorities' radar, zipping through the traffic circle where they checked for more than two people per boda, driver included. In an attempt to dodge detection our driver headed for the sidewalk, but we were suddenly vice pinched in between two taxi vans, with contact on both shoulders.

Our driver honked and yelled something which shot us into a clearing. He crossed a three-lane street, with my hand touching the grills of each of the cars we pulled in front of and we were back at E-tower.

Gone from our lookout post for just under an hour we dashed up to Steve's office. After wasting time chasing down a make-believe lead, we wanted to make sure Mr. Slippery didn't make an appearance without being snared. The secretary and the assistant were huddled over her desk intently discussing something when we came in. Just then, her phone rang and the assistant invited us out into the elevator area.

I was the first to lay into the assistant weasel's deer-in-the-headlights look, threatening going to the police, exposing him, his boss and the whole business unless he got us something solid instead of bad information, stalling and lies. My finger tapping his shirt buttons, nearly drilling a hole through his chest to his spineless backside.

"My humble apologies, please, and I am most embarrassed to work for such a crooked man," he confessed. "But it is the only job I have to make any money to help feed my family and I hope you would understand. He told me to tell you to go to the embassy to waste some time while he worked something out.

Both the secretary and I are threatening to quit and go to the police ourselves unless he tells us where the birth certificate is. I believe we are close."

It was 3 p.m. I couldn't see much being salvaged before our looming departure. The weekend government schedules would shut down any last hopes. My mind was reeling so fast with any last ditch efforts that I didn't even notice Nita trailing the assistant back into the law office.

The secretary put her nail file down and without even looking at Nita, opened the top drawer of her desk. She said she just got a text from Steve and he gave her permission to hand it out. She slowly reached down inches from where she had been sitting the last three days in a locked stare-down with Nita, and pulled out the birth certificate from the center drawer.

Nita had a glazed over, mannequin-like look as she came out from Lawyer Steve's office with the words "advocate" over it. Wordlessly, she handed me a narrow, half-sheet piece of paper with red borders and lettering. I read the names on the document.

In the square where it listed William's legal nearest relative was our double agent assistant. I wasn't sure if I was relieved to get the paper, incensed that it seemed to be a now-legal fakery, or be grateful that he pounced on a grenade for us.

Now we needed more that just an advocate, we needed someone who could turn this mini-manuscript into a major last-second miracle.

The realization sunk in that we were starting completely over at what should have been the finish line. I turned and barreled down the flight of stairs toward another advocate sign on the floor below.

As I skipped the last step, the light in the office revealed a Muslim scarf-framed woman just below a computer monitor, and a man at a desk hovering over a stack of file folders.

I bowled in, nearly knocking over the startled secretary with the crash I made pushing the door open.

"Is this an honest law firm?" I said. "Are you a good lawyer?"

"Yes I am," he said, standing up. He pulled down his glasses off a befuddled, but serious face.

"What I mean by 'good' is: Are you an honest lawyer or will you rip me off like the guy upstairs did?"

"I am not like that man upstairs," he said.

He extended his hand humbly toward my accusing finger. We slowly shook hands. It was the first time I realized that my forceful efforts weren't going to matter. I couldn't make things right, right now.

"My name is Mungoma Justin. I am a man of my word, and I will do everything that I say."

Choking back the tears of anguish I said, "And I will pay you what your word is worth. I need a man of integrity and I need a miracle."

"I can help you," he said. "Please sit down."

I slumped back into a chair. And started from the bottom.

Like a man at the bottom of an elevator shaft.

10

MIRACLE WEEKEND

An Argentinean cattle rancher once told me a story that started like this:

"I don't believe in miracles, but there are some."

He told an elaborate story about some boyhood friend of his who was lame from birth. Somewhere around the kid's seventh birthday, the mother heard from a long-haul trucker who shuttled cattle off the ranch, that if she put her crippled boy inside of a freshly slaughtered cow's stomach for a half hour, the lameness would be cured.

Desperation can be a despicable adversary. On behalf of someone you love, many of us would try just about anything. Desperation can also bring into play situations that can only be described as the workings of God. Bonafide miracles.

Our new lawyer Justin went right to the metal shelving unit just behind me and pulled down two Ugandan law books. Silently he flipped the pages to the two he was searching. He rubbed his clean-shavened face for a moment before turning them toward me to examine.

"You must have legal guardianship to take a minor out of the country," he said pressing his finger on the pages. "You also cannot get a passport without having legal guardianship. You could only apply for a passport if you were a family member applying on behalf of the child. So, you will need a court date to gain this guardianship or you will not get what you need."

It felt like the final nail in the coffin. The questions piled up in my mind. Did we get this wrong? Does God not want us to continue? Did Nita just fly off the handle with her emotions and now reality has gaveled a verdict? We were at a new level of defeat. Knowing the amount of time it takes to get a court date in the states, my first thought was that this would take years.

"Can you call the court right now and see when the next date is?" I asked.

He pulled his mobile phone out of his pressed shirt pocket and turned toward the wall. Nita, William and the pastor were just filing in after figuring out where the heck I ran off to. By the look on her face I could tell that she didn't find the crooked lawyer.

Justin put his hand over the phone and relayed the first bit of bad news. The court clerk told him they were backed up for six months. Also there was a scheduled recess that following Monday, and further, child cases were only seen on Tuesdays and Thursdays. As Justin was speaking English to us, I could hear the clerk through the phone doing some Lugandan negotiations.

"I am sorry Mr. and Mrs. (he didn't even know our last name yet), but this doesn't look good. You two may have to go back home and return at a later date," Justin said.

He abruptly put his hand up for room silence, to listen to the phone that was at his ear.

"Mmmmm," he mumbled. Then again. And again. "Mmmmm, ah ha, mmmm."

This went on for what seemed like three minutes before he pressed the end button.

"It seems you may have your miracle," he said, grinning slightly. "The clerk said you may see the judge on

Tuesday, at 11a.m. We mustn't be late, and we have a lot to do before then. So let us move quickly."

The four of us erupted with relief. The news brought in fresh hope, but also took us deeper into a quarry of keeping our promise to William.

I went down to the money exchange kiosk at the street level to trade off the last of our cash resources. Another million schillings to the table. Nita had just gotten off the phone to the airlines to delay our departure. I knew the reading of my credit card number meant something expensive. Yep, another thousand dollars to the airlines.

Yet the exhilaration of getting something done and now being right in the midst of a God-given miracle pushed us forward without regard to the costs. "If it's God's will, it's God's bill," we kept telling ourselves.

However, for the weekend in waiting, Nita was not going to have any part of the single-sheet guest house with the steel doors and the "make love" shower spigot.

"If I'm going to survive this, I'm going to need an upgrade," she said. "I can't do one more day at that place let alone the entire next week."

Between E-tower and the Sheraton on the hill was a pretty good place called the Hotel Triangle. It offered a large bed with sheets, a comforter, hot shower with water pressure, TV and air conditioning. A slice of heaven in the inner city. It even had a swimming pool. Funny, because hardly anybody in Africa knows how to swim.

On the advice of the pastor, he would stay with William in the house of one of his relatives. Again, we were trying to thwart the rumor mill that could scuttle our intentions. Fortunately, the hotel took credit cards for our room, another thousand dollars for the week was pinged on my numbers. But at least we got a decent night's sleep.

With a full weekend ahead of us to kill before court, we bled our story out to all our friends and family back in the states. On top of the prayers, encouraging words and suggestions of tactics, one of the US2Uganda4Life people gave us the phone number of a guy who was in the inner circles of the political hub. According to her reports, he was able to get their ministry idea to build and operate medical clinics all the way to the vice president of the country. Quickly after, he requested a personal meeting with her, intercepting the group at the airport before they left on their last mission trip.

His name was "Bob Fitness." That wasn't his real name, but it was an American pseudonym he used as a name and a brand. Supposedly, he used some stateside athletic-type contacts to woo change and policy in Africa. We were told he was a stand-up guy and got things done. It was worth a few mobile minutes to find out.

As a sign of possible divine providence again, he was in town and was staying at the Sheraton just up the hill from us. He agreed to see us at the garden sports bar between some "high level" meetings he said he was having.

Nita and I briskly walked up the hill and waited in the empty bar for about ten minutes before a beefy, broad shouldered man waltzed in. He had a noticeably heavy ego and a make-believe entourage. Soon, Bob's tale of his American friends and high society Ugandan associates and great feats of good were unveiled like a billboard of baloney.

That said, I figured if the guy could say a word or two that would get William out of the country by the very next Saturday, I was willing to wade through the deepest of bat guano and prop up his self-importance in exchange.

We gave him the two-minute highlights—or, more accurately, lowlights—of our predicament. Because we shared a common American friend whom the vice president now liked immensely, he seemed more than eager to help. It also made him look good to be involved and aiding the Muzungu's who were aiding the country. Politically, rubbing elbows with Americans doing aid in country seemed like a status thing. Something that was best when milked.

"I am free for a bit Monday morning before I head back out of town," he said. "We should meet again. By then, my people will be back at their work posts and, if need be, we can go and speak to them directly."

We bought his soda, thanked him for his time, and got the power handshake and another short tale starring Bob Fitness. Nita and I strolled down the hill, hand in hand, buoyed a little more to our new-found favor and the soon-to-be benefits to our networking. We looked at this as another open door of God doing what He does, so we continued to walk through.

Sunday morning we slept in past the hotel's breakfast time. I remembered seeing a sign at the Sheraton about a Sunday brunch. Still having no cash until we could draw some out against our VISA card, we headed back up the hill. The was a buffet of overpriced eggs benedict with an African twist topped with pineapple garnish.

At first impression, our wardrobe was a tad under the Sunday suit and dress code. I had a dri-fit black shirt on with a pair of travel shorts with the legs zipped on, so technically they were long pants. Nita wore a pair of white crops, leather flip-flops and a University of Oregon Duck, green and yellow, football v-neck.

With the first load of food freight on my plate, I began the sweep of the veranda to find where Nita was sitting. Across the room I could see she was talking to an American-looking woman about the same age. Seated with her were a few others, including one guy with a very colorfully grand, extravagant robe outfit.

With my curio meter now pegged, I reached the table just as the woman says she's from the northwest and loves the University of Oregon Ducks. After she spied out Nita's shirt she made a "go Ducks" comment just about the time Nita walked by the table, instantly striking up a conversation.

Turns out they were a non-profit, medical type group from the U.S. doing clinic set-ups in the kingdom province of Uganda. Looking around the room, it seemed like we had fallen into the banquet of the "who's who" of the international aid groups. There were a smattering of Muzungu's from all countries, government official-looking Ugandans and a sharply suited businessman.

"So what brings you to Uganda?," the woman sitting across the guy wearing the coat of many colors said. "Are you part of an aid work or what's your story?"

There was a long "well" and then an extended sigh from Nita, followed by the detailed events of our ordeal trying to get William to the states. The colorful guy sitting across from the lady seemed most interested in the discussion and made some signal.

"Oh, I'm sorry," the woman interrupted. "Please let me introduce you to the Prince of Buganda."

Now, before I go further, networking seems to follow Nita and I wherever we go. The joke among our friends is that we cannot go anywhere without seeing someone we know, or have done business with or have crossed paths in some way. And with that, favor seems to be closely behind each of these sets of connections.

Buganda is the region right in the middle of Uganda that was once part of on old tribal kingdom subsequently taken over by a former dictatorship regime. Just recently, under the current president, it had been re-instituted to its former monarchy with all of the rights including its former independence. It was now kind of like an independent country slash kingdom in the middle of a country. Coincidently, this area was governed by a prince, who also had jurisdiction over Kampala, which included the court system we were trying to gain a miracle from in the next week. It was that prince who was sitting at this table.

"Your story touches my heart," the Prince said. "I believe we can offer some help."

Instantly I'm thinking God has delivered the miracle guy right into our laps—on a weekend no less! One phone call and the prince guy could have William on a plane with a VISA stamp on a fresh passport and us out of there—but there was more. As we kept learning, there's always more.

"You say you are a dental person and have worked in clinics with American missionaries," he prodded. "Tell me how we as a kingdom can set up clinics with people of your expertise to help our people."

The conversation swayed to his needs and how Nita could use her influence to help, in exchange of course, for help with William.

"I would have traded just about anything at that moment to get us the passport and guardianship," she later said.

The prince and his staff said they would make some calls the following morning. As the info exchange was coming to a close, the very refined, three-piece-suited gentleman, who no doubt had heard the goings on, came over. The prince introduced him and praised him as the "best lawyer in Kampala" and reviewed with him the highlights of story.

"Ah, I know exactly what judge you will see on Tuesday. I've known him for years, he is a good friend of mine," the Armani-clad attorney said. "Surely I will tell him of your dealings with the crooked lawyer and see if I can help get you what you desire."

We were ecstatic! Favor with a one-two punch. The top prince and the top attorney. Surely with those two voices, our state of international affairs was in the bag. Monday couldn't come soon enough for the avalanche of great fortune we'd been swept into at this chance champagne brunch.

We all parted ways with the proverbial, "We'll be in touch at the latest tomorrow afternoon."

It turned out to be a great weekend for miracles.

By the way, the trucker from Argentina telling the story of the lame kid who walked after being in the cow's stomach for a half hour—he was that boy. The same guy who didn't believe in miracles but believed there are some, was the walking testament to a large one.

Although we didn't have to go near a cow's stomach to get our miracle, it sure seemed that, to reach our Promised Land, we were wading through an awful lot of what comes out the other end.

11

TRUTH IS.

Truth is. What you do in a situation where the option is either.

Truth is. When nobody would be the wiser, what course of action do you take that is the wisest for your own gain?

Truth is. That if Nita and I ever decided to be a couple of small-time, little-white liars, the jinx would be thoroughly known in a very wide network in pretty short order. That's both the beauty and the bane of attracting attention with high-powered people who are promising to help.

Truth is, during a test of honesty and integrity, truth is what a person falls back to, not what they believe they would do the next time.

As I get older, it becomes ever clearer to me that any past contact has the potential to become a future asset in hundreds of situations. Integrity becomes the calling card that opens doors and keeps them open. We've experienced this over and again. Doors that would have slammed shut in our faces, or smacked us in the butt going out, aren't worth the risk when trying to pull some kind of deception for quick gain.

So it goes without saying that this miraculous line-up of good fortune that followed us to the buffet table put us on high anticipation of goodness to come. Call it a breakthrough, skilled networking, an approachable spirit, or not being afraid to ask for help in desperate situations. Whatever, it was a major momentum shift going into the new week.

We had chosen to take William out of the country on our own accord. Without going through the normal channels of an adoption agency (because we believed our case was easier and less red tape bringing him back as a student). In doing so, we inadvertently raised trafficking flag within the Ugandan system as an untested case. Any situation that looks somewhat "special" raises colossal concern. So all of our sudden, high-powered attention (that we were unknowingly focusing on one child) sent a message before us that we had no idea was actually fighting against us. Our miracle was being steadily thwarted by the network of people wanting to help.

Many times through this process, we looked at each other and questioned our sanity why we didn't quit. But Nita was unequivocally convinced that's why God chose us. I hate quitting, just as much as Nita hates losing.

Blindly confident, though, we pressed headlong into the coming week. As any typical Ugandan Monday morning started, it began to unfold eventually around lunch time. We had an 11 a.m. meeting with Bob Fitness regarding a little greasing of the officials. The pastor and William picked us up in front of Hotel Triangle and we threaded our way up the hill to the Sheraton, to pick up Mr. Fitness.

"I will need a little more money to talk to these officials," fast-talkin' Bob said the moment he got into the truck. "With these government-type employees it takes some expenses for them to gain assistance from others in the office to get things done quickly."

"About how much are we talking here?" I asked. "If I pay more money, will that get the passport?"

Instantly suspicious, I shelved it, believing even this was all part of the miracle process. We'd already given Bob $50 to make the initial appointment, so I was struggling to see what this new amount was for.

We pulled along the sidewalk of a four-lane thoroughfare in front of a strip of warehouse looking buildings. There were lines of people everywhere and about half a block ahead, I caught a glimpse of a sign that read, "Passport Office." Bob stepped out of the truck and told us all to wait. It was scorching hot. We sat under a roadside tree so we could watch the vehicle.

Fitness headed inside the compound, striding like he owned the place. He walked right past the hundreds of people in line, right through the security gate without as much as pausing, and disappeared around the corner.

Ten minutes went by. The pastor reassured us business is done this way and results would happen very soon. Another twenty minutes went by. Nita and I, sitting with the young William, were attracting some attention. The looks from the bystanders made me edgy. I felt like we were being sized up, talked about, scrutinized and judged.

After nearly an hour, big Bob, who towered over the locals by a foot, whistled and waved at us to come toward the security gate. By the time we got there he was speaking heatedly with the officers holding out his official governmental I.D. badge with one hand and with his other hand waved us in.

The place was buzzing with people standing and sitting along the walls of the various offices. There was a makeshift theater, roped over with a blue tarp covering a dozen chairs from the sun showing a video about leaving the country. Signs plastered everywhere warned of falsifying documents, wrong forms that would delay processing and dozens of posters with alerts about child traffickers.

Bob leapt up onto the one-stair porch where a few

people were sitting a few inches above the dirt courtyard and barreled into office number 103. It was barely a tiny closet in a row of government cubicles with people swarming around each entryway like it was a garage sale. Two clerks were seated behind two worn out desks, devoid of drawers and lacquer. Balanced along the walls surrounding the room were four tiers of shelves with file folders bulging with loose papers, all string tied and stacked higher than any of the clerks could reach.

An abrupt hush fell onto the room when we all squeezed in. Bob's voice boomed over all of the chaos to the clerk with the sweaty armpits closest to the door. They exchanged sharply. The officials' eyes bounced back and forth, looking at us, then William, then vocally sparring with Bob, then back at us.

The dusty desk man patted through some folders piled on his workstation and pulled out William's near the bottom. More sharp words to Bob were exchanged. Before we knew it, we were whisked out of the office.

We never exactly found out what was spoken to the passport guy, but at least we saw that William's file was near his desk, within direct reach of the process, and that was somewhat hopeful.

On the way out of the courtyard, Bob was bragging about how much influence he had. He said the issuance of the passport would happen right after the court awarded us a legal guardianship the next day. But, in order to make sure, he asked a third time, for "a little more money."

Don't get me wrong, we were still desperate, but we weren't getting stupider. I flatly refused. Explaining to Mr. Big Shot that in my country, results are paid for not with promises, but with results. Based on the closing conversational tone in the office, I was having second-guessing checks about him in my gut.

Bob Fitness shrugged off my posturing and said he would catch a motor-cycle taxi to his next appointment. He walked the opposite way of the parked truck just about the time a white uniformed police officer was writing us a parking ticket.

Tuesday morning, third floor of the child welfare court building, 8:30 am., we were early and ready for our 9 a.m. docket.

William's mother was to meet us that morning in the front of the court building via motorcycle taxi. We even told her to be there an hour ahead of when we needed her, just to make sure. As we were walking up to the entrance gate, we found her waiting outside with her three-month old baby girl in tow, wrapped up in the blanket that Nita had given her a few days earlier.

We went upstairs to the waiting room. A few other white people with dark kids started too, all sharply dressed either in suits or dresses, clutching little Ugandan kids dressed like baby Gap ads. It made me nervous. All we had on was our best tourist garb.

William wore his white zip-up jacket, with red and blue arm stripes over a solid shirt and some new jeans. He was the oldest kid in that room by more than ten years. I felt either out of place or different. We were banking on different, because our case wasn't about adoption. We were just there to get a kid to come to the U.S. for an education.

Across the hall and down a door was an adjoining room between the two judges' chambers. Packed mostly with suited male lawyers but also a few smartly attired women, it was like a boiler room for attorneys. They jockeyed their positions to be seen either with "the foul" one or the woman judge, who was the one everybody seemed to want.

As luck would have it, our appointment was with the "foul one." He had not only arrived late, but the case ahead of us lingered on and on.

While we waited in the holding room we heard a handful of other people's stories, nightmares really. One couple had been in the city for over six weeks wading through the process. They had rented an apartment, called back and put their stateside jobs on hold. It was their third trip back. The husband had to fly out in a few days, leaving the wife to finish up the last legalities of getting a passport and VISA stamp on her own. Glad that wasn't going to be us.

Those little brown toddlers were climbing on the other couples laps pining for hugs and snacks. We on the other hand, had a pre-teenager pacing about the room, somewhat disconnected and certainly not cooing at our side. We even received some brave admiration from those with the little kids for taking on someone older. I assured them though, we were just there for educational purposes, to help for a while, we weren't thinking of putting William in our will or anything.

These couples from every corner of the states were in it so deep, yet the submergence hadn't drowned them. Instead, I observed first hand, that it had brought out strengths and promise-keeping they'd never thought was in their character. These pursuits for these kids were becoming the largest stories of their lives.

What was also true: Theses couples had savvy adoption attorneys who had been down this apparent pot-holed road before. Because of that familiarity, they were getting cycled through the woman judge fairly quickly. Justin was a land-use attorney, this pond was all new. He holed up in the boiler room trying to secure a place in line before lunch. He even tried to maneuver our case onto the woman judge to avoid the "foul one" in hopes of a speedy and favorable ruling.

Noontime came and went, along with our 11 a.m. appointment. Justin came and poked his head inside the holding room entry.

"I think the judge is going to see you just before lunchtime," Justin said right about the time the judge's hungry mass walked behind him, carrying a brown bag.

"Perhaps we should go and get some lunch then," he said. "If we go now, we can come back in time."

At this point, Nita and I were on long-haul, stakeout mentality. We weren't going anywhere. So we gave some money to Justin and the Pastor to bring us back a candy bar and some juice. It was grasshopper season and I didn't want to get a bag of French-fried field bugs. With our stomachs tied in knots, we were getting the idea of how the place ran and how a missed moment could spell disaster.

Finally, late in the afternoon, it was our turn. We hustled down the hall and ducked through the crowded lawyers in the boiler room, thick with stale body odor. Filing through a doorway to the left, and then inside the judge's office, was a scene right out of Star Wars. At first glance was a guy who when seated, looked like Jabba the Hut. It was of course, the judge, the foul one, plopped behind a very large wooden desk, ringed in his layers of fat.

The man had a booming voice and a flour-frosted head of short-cropped hair. His throne was a roughly finished high back leather chair situated among a grand room of legal props and books. Behind the throne, bone and steel war weapons hung on the wall.

We barely got inside before he announced the confrontations were about to begin. We stood tensely for an awkwardly long period while all the Lugandan language introduction went on. Justin relayed some of it in English, then gave us the OK to sit. He handed the woman court reporter our file, sat in one of the hot seats in front and went right into the presentation. The court reporter numbly flipped over the file and in a few seconds, dished it over to Jabba.

He peered over his half rimmed magnifier glasses and finger-waved to the empty chair in front of the desk next to Justin. Justin in turn motioned for me to upgrade from coach, to first class sizzle seat.

"So you are trying to get a student visa for this boy William Biyinzika?" the judge said.

"Yes we are, my lord," I said sticking to my TV education from the last legal show I'd watched.

"This is a great opportunity for the young boy, so tell me where will he go to school and where will he live while he is under your care?" He looked past me and now over to Nita.

"Well he will live with us and go to a private, Christian school that we have already secured an F-1 VISA from," Nita said from the perimeter seats. "He would live with us and we would take him to school every morning and pick him up in the afternoon. He would have his own room in our home as well."

The judge turned instantly confused.

"Why would you do this?" he said firing questions back at Nita. "Why would you take the boy to school and pick him up everyday? And why would he live with you when he could live at the school?"

"Well your honor," Nita explained. "In America, we don't do a boarding school situation. Our children live with the family and the family takes the responsibility to get the child back and forth to school."

"Mmmmm, mmm," he grumbled.

"But you two are." He looked over his glasses toward me and then back to my 51-year old bottle-blond wife. "How do I put this? You are so old." the judge said, cracking the slightest grin, which triggered periphery chuckles from the rest of the nervous congregation.

Buoyed by the humor, I felt like everything was going to come together in the next few moments. The "foul one" was sweetening up. He was even seeing the great benefit of us taking William right now. He has to know we're not bad people, I thought. Just pick up the gavel and pound us out of here.

He continued to warm asking more details about us and our grown kids. He asked in a round about way, why we would do something like this when we were "nearing the good time of your life," as he put it.

"I believe this is what God has called us to do," Nita responded faithfully. "And I don't believe in fighting against God."

That statement hit some serious pay dirt, because the judge murmured something to the effect that he didn't want to buck God either.

He turned to the mother. He quizzed her about permission, asked her if we had offered her any money or made her promises for taking William. He also grilled the pastor on William's history at Jireh and the time line pertaining to the death of his father. He then summed up his thoughts back to Justin, cloaking them in Lugandan.

It's like a language switch. If you're not supposed to be in on the conversation, it's the native tongue, if you are, it bounces back to English. Most Ugandans speak decent English.

The judge collated the papers and tapped them vertically on his desk to neatly fit back into the file.

"Two things I need before I can help you with this opportunity. First, I need more paperwork," he said, shaking his judgment finger at us. He held the file like a pizza, weighing it with the other hand, "and I will also need someone representing the father's side of the boy to come here and give approval. There needs to be no division among the boys remaining family members.

"I want to help you out with this because it is such a good opportunity for this young man. You come back with what I ask and I will see you Thursday at 11a.m. so you can have time get the VISA. You will need an uncle or a direct relative from the father, so go hurry and get somebody."

He banged the wooden hammer. Justin abruptly sat

up and, in a few moments of commotion, motioned for all of us to herd quickly on out of chambers back to the holding area. There he laid down the next move in our miracle case.

"Beings you say that the father died when the boy was very young, it may be nearly impossible to track down a direct relative now," Justin said, obviously frustrated.

"We don't have enough time to search all over the country and to get some relative back here by Thursday morning. I think you may have to come back and finish this at a later date. It might not be possible now."

"Not," I pleaded, with my desperate, I'll-be-damned-if-I'm-quitting defiance. "There's got to be something we can do. We've been given the miracle of another court date. That's two in the same week! We've got to get somebody back here, a person the judge will accept."

The pastor slipped in to our discussion. "We could find someone who knows William's mother and pay him to say he is one of the father's brothers. It would take just a little money and it would serve what the judge wants. That's how it's done here."

I'm sure he meant well, but it was as if a serpent had spun out of the ceiling fan to slither out a convenient and also corrupt solution.

In other words, he was saying, we would take some guy off the street, stage him with the story, feed him some lines, make him out to be an uncle. It would allow us to give the necessary testimony we needed. To cross this boundary, you justify telling a lie for the greater good. This puts an already unstable foot in the swiftest of waters because never know where that lie is going to take you.

Truth is, we were, again, nearly out of time even with this extension of our trip. Truth is, we had to decide to use this "made-up" guy to bear false witness in the glaring Exodus 20:16 kind of way. Truth is, the birth certificate in front of the judge had a crooked attorney's aid as the next of kin. All of the sudden, I could see a tangled rabbit trail of lies open up before us like a black hole with this temptation of efficiency sucking us all down into itself.

There was an anesthetizing silence. Right before one's soul is asphyxiated to choose the real right from the justifiable and convenient choice of what *looks* right. My insides were screaming to avenge back the bad we've been dealt. I was searching for an excuse to the morality of choosing this charade. But as much as I wanted to say something either for or against, my mouth couldn't utter anything.

I flashbacked to how I busted into Justin's office and demanded an honest lawyer. What would I say now after all that? Not to mention the way he was looking at me, with a piercing kind of intensity. He too, was waiting for my next word that would either be the defining pillar of who I claimed to be or a lying hypocrite.

"We won't lie," Nita said firmly before I could speak. "We can't be part of a growing lie. I won't lie. I won't make up a relative. I won't crush the process or be a part of the corruption.

"I have to know that every step is a step from God. If dishonesty and desperation take us to the point of the final closed door, then we will do it honestly. If not, none of us will know where this should have led or could have gone. I would rather bear the weight of the truth than the cost of the other.

"Besides, if we get caught, then it's done," she said amid tears. "We'll never know if we did all God wanted. William will never go home."

"William will never go home?" My mind reeled. I ran that phrase over and over again in my mind feeling for the first time the real gravity of that sentiment. Home. William part of our home? It was enormous.

William kept up the interpretation with his mom right up to home part at the end. Regina, with a spark of determination, said she had a plan. She said there was a half uncle who was once a part of the tribe his father was connected to. The local tribal elder in her province of Kampala would know of his whereabouts and she was certain she could get him to court by Thursday morning. We gave some boda-boda money for her and for the uncle to return, and she left in a hurry.

"We will hope the mother finds the uncle and brings him back," Justin said, latching his briefcase closed. "Because that is our last hope for getting William his VISA. I bid you good day."

Truth is, Justin didn't want to lie either. Even with the pastor's blessing. Truth is, we still had a number of people who hadn't contacted the judge that I still believed would help us out. I knew also Regina had a mother's desire for William to go to school in America. She would do anything to see that come to pass.

Truth is, I had to trust that her word about the uncle was genuine, and that he could be proved as a solid family relative.

Truth is, with the judge's decision, we had just started to fall backward, not knowing how far we would plunge, into the hands of God.

12

THE BOTTOM FALLS OUT, AGAIN

Truth is like propane.

When there's a faithful supply of fuel, there's plenty of light. Without it, the flame goes "poof" and darkness prevails. It reminded me of the fire pit in our back yard when the tank runs out of gas.

The decision against lying to produce a relative was the best decision. The next morning, a Wednesday, we received phone calls from those who made commitments to help, to confirm in fact, they'd made those pleas on our behalf. We thanked them profusely, and updated them of our progress. Several remarked about our integrity.

"Keep up the honest work, and God will prevail," the female assistant to the Prince said. "Our thoughts and prayers are with you. This judge now understands who you are and what you want to do."

My prayers and thoughts were banking that this uncommon influence would put a fire under judge Jabba before our next hearing. We were burning up precious time. If many more temptations were going to be coming my way, I had better be looking for some more propane.

We disliked the situation with William staying in some skanky room across town with the pastor's relatives, we brought him into Hotel Triangle with us. He slept on a stack of pillows lined up at the foot of our bed under the extra blanket. We figured that with as many people who knew about us and our intentions, potentially sordid rumors wouldn't gain any traction.

That Thursday, we got to the court building with enough time to secure an off-street parking space. Walking a block down and around the corner, we saw Regina with the baby and a slender man about her same height standing obviously close.

She introduced him through William's interpreting. I couldn't tell you his name to save my life, but it didn't matter anyway. He just needed to be an actual branch of this messy, multi-rooted tree. And he apparently was.

O the third floor were the same faces, same routine, different day. At 10:45 a.m., 15 minutes before our appointment, there was no sign of the judge.

"The court reporter wants 50,000 schillings for her to give your file to the judge so he will see you," Justin told us.

Nita and I exploded in sync. Both of us shot back comments that she could just do her job and put our file in the lineup because the judge promised to see us in fifteen minutes.

"Nobody gets another dime out of me," Nita protested. "I have paid out enough money to everyone around here. She'll not get any of my money. I have an appointment with a judge he gave us for crying out loud, and it's at 11."

"You will not see the judge today at all if we do not pay her what she's asking."

Just on principle I was sticking to "no." And I said it a few dozen times in the rant which followed. But somewhere in those sideline moments, Nita slipped Justin the money while I was on the other side of the room. Our lawyer quietly went on about his business.

The mid-morning came and went. That nebulous lunch time between 11am and 2:30 also slipped away from us. The uncle sat nearly motionless in the corner chair for the entire morning and then into the afternoon.

Across the hall and over the wall-top windows the judge continued his legal tongue-lashing to the first-case people. I must have looked at my watch a thousand times trying to calculate if we still had enough time to get the VISA approval from the court, run to get the passport office before they closed at 4 p.m., then somehow make our flight at midnight on Saturday, the day after.

At one point Justin came out of the boiler room and said, "You guys all need to pray. Pray right now, and pray hard, because this judge is very angry today and is yelling at the family ahead of you."

Without notice, in the mid-afternoon around 3:30, the judge just disappeared. It was like a governmental version of hide and seek. Many of us thought he went on a bathroom break, but a stall search turned up nothing. So for about 90 unexplained minutes, there was no flush, no sign, no judge. No progress.

Rays of gold spilled into the western facing waiting room from the far horizon throwing shadows of doom across the wall. My watch reconfirmed the bad news: the passport office just closed. It was 4 p.m. An overwhelming sense of helpless emptiness had just dismantled my walls of optimism. Pessimism was building as I heard the judge back in his chambers bellowing new orders, taking more time.

I blamed the court reporter who stacked the file. I blamed perfume lady because she was the only one who smelled like she could afford it. I also blamed the crooked lawyer. I blamed myself for not being smarter. I stopped just before blaming my wife. I walked over and kissed her.

"It has to be only God now," I said. "Because nothing we can do will change anything at this point."

She was fragmented and fatigued way beyond the faked smile she forced out. Her deep worry was seeping its way to the surface. Through her eyes, I could see the slippage of her losing heart. Losing hope.

Five p.m. came and ticked by. Five thirty. The yelling coming from the chambers had pretty much stopped. The building had cleared out, along with any likelihood of a miracle.

Justin, for the last number of hours, had positioned himself in the doorway of the judge's office on a chair. His elbows had indented his thighs and he had twiddled his thumbs to mere stubs. Every time the feisty gray-haired ruler glanced over his bifocals to spit some venom at the defendants in his chambers, he was forced to make eye contact with our lawyer. There was one more case to see today, and we weren't about to give up. Apparently, Justin hated to lose as much as I did.

It was six o'clock when the initial weary dozen that had taken all of the judge's time and energy for the entire day, finally departed. We stuffed ourselves into the outer chambers, crowding the doorway.

Before the judge could get up and stretch, Justin handed the slightly thicker file to perfume lady who passed it right to the judge who was gathering his coat. I guess this is what you get for fifty thousand schillings. Like a jelly fish, he refilled the chair and reluctantly opened our file.

He gestured to the uncle and didn't even call him to the hot seat in front of the desk. At this time of day, every seat around the perimeter was an official testimony platform.

The uncle answered a few questions to the whereabouts of the birth father's side of the family, asserting that all of them were dispersed and disconnected. Regina filled in the details of how her subsequent marriage to a Muslim man, years ago, complicated William having a family. The pastor asked to speak and added some further information between the time William came to the orphanage shortly after Regina's marriage to the present. It all seemed to satisfy the judge's requests.

He flipped the file to the back and made some notes. Twisting over his right shoulder in his rolling chair the judge barked something at the assistant near the bookcase, who quickly produced a hefty law book and laid it before him.

Just before he cracked the book's binding, the judge paused and looked at us.

"Let me tell you what kind of judge I am," he began. His furry eyebrows burrowed down on both of us. He picked up a small ruler, just to move it out of his way, but for a minute I thought he was going to smack both of our hands with it.

"I am a judge who upholds the law as it is laid down in my country. I will not be persuaded or swayed to the likes of different people calling me, urging me on what I should do on a matter, before I've even heard it." He hammered the point home with a stern stare to all of us then, as the crickets chirped, he laid a longer stare just to me.

The temperature in the room was steadily rising, like his tone.

"I don't know who you people think you are, but I do not appreciate outsiders meddling in the matters of my court. No one is going to try and tell me what I should do for people they know. That kind of tactic will not help you."

From that moment on, the demolition and crumbling began. All that miraculous networking and connections were about to bite us in the butt and leave a large scar. Indeed, all of those people who had promised had made good, but the "foul one" wasn't one to be won over by influence from friends.

Licking two fingers, he curled past the corners of several pages in the law book on his desk until he came to the right section. He read aloud the legalese from the reference book.

"According to the codes and rules of our land, I see no laws concerning taking a minor out of the country for educational reasons," he said. Justin, who was now stone-faced, squirmed noticeably. I got the sense he knew what was coming, and was bracing for impact.

"Besides, this file is still too thin." He said that a number of times while getting to the main point. "I want this young man to have this opportunity but we need more from you two. The law requires that you have Legal Guardianship first before you can take a minor out of the country. The only laws I have are for adoptions. There is nothing here for taking a child away strictly for educational purposes. So those that are written are the laws I must uphold."

"You both will have to go back to the U.S. and get me enough to give you legal guardianship. Then and only then can I help this young man with this opportunity."

For a split second, the judge appeared to have a heart. I was miffed though. I felt the judge could have let us slide with some dang grace. In my interpretation, we were doing more with the "spirit" of the law than he was by sticking to its "letter." The "letter" is what did us in. Well, that and all of those people—with the best of intentions—calling to convince him otherwise.

Just before the judge slid out from under his desk to hastily leave, Nita called back to him with one final question.

"Are you requiring that both of us come back here into court or can just one of us come and fulfill these requirements?" she asked.

"No, one person is fine," he said. "Just one of you can come back in a few months and we will have this all worked out."

It was just before seven when the balloon was officially deflated beyond repair. Regina hugged my wife and spoke some foreign reassurance to her.

Justin gave us both his condolences. He said he would begin working right away on the Legal Guardianship. I asked if I could give him some more money to help with the filing expenses and he reluctantly took a few hundred thousand schillings. We promised to be in regular contact via e-mail to plan the next date to return. On his way off the third floor, he gave Nita a hug and apologized. Seeing the tears already beginning to drain from her face, he apologized again.

Looking out the windows from the holding room, I could see gridlock in the streets below. There was a midnight flight through Amsterdam to Portland on Thursdays, the same leg we had tickets on for Saturday. I figured if we made a decision right now and caught tonight's flight, we could get home quicker to get back sooner. In my mind every minute counted. There was no question which one of us was coming back, but if it was up to me, the "when" would be as soon as possible.

Later, William would say that what hurt him most was Nita and I having to waste a lot of money and time. He was still confident either Nita or I would be back for him—and shocked to think he was returning to his old school after having said goodbye to everyone.

With the sense of dire urgency to get back home and start the paperwork, we threw what money we had left to the pastor to re-buy all of Williams school supplies so he could be put back into Jireh school.

Checking online, we saw the next flight out had two seats left on it, desperately we convinced the pastor to face the late evening gridlock to get us to the airport.

We weren't able to think thing completely through on the drive out of the city, but we felt grateful that William was going to be in good hands to transition back into a holding pattern for the meantime. The rushing about also made the awkwardness of a long goodbye less painful when we weren't having to face it head on.

In the parking lot, Nita embraced William—and braced for the inevitable. I tried to make may farewell brief as I pulled the bags out of the pickup bed, selfishly trying to spare my ragged emotions. Nita waved while running backward as I led the forward charge up the airport ramp while leashed with the bags.

We were first in line and first through security only to be politely told by the ticket counter lady that the flight was overbooked. We would have to wait our flight, on Saturday. Sorry.

We hung our heads once again and hailed a taxi to a nearby airport hotel, where we crashed for the night, after calling the pastor and arranging a morning rendezvous.

It turned out to be a blessing in disguise. Besides getting to see William for a few more days, we learned he didn't want to go back to his old Jireh school. And that led to something better.

He had already said his "good-byes" and gave away all his stuff. To go back now would "just not be good." I got it. Awkward. Repeated explanations. He doesn't like long goodbyes either, chip off the old block.

We pulled into Brian and Angela's compound in Masaka with faces of defeat and lots of detailed explaining. Angela more theatrical in her receiving of the news, Brian was noticeably stoic from the news of the crooked lawyer carnage.

Within the first hour however, we had a band-aid plan. The two of them phoned a new friend who was the director of the best private boarding school in the area. They arranged an appointment to get William in. They prenegotiated a good price and helped us get a list of the specific supplies we needed. To make us feel better, they also volunteered their home for weekend sleepovers with William so that we could SKYPE chat with him every Saturday. This way we could stay connected emotionally, he could play with their kids, they could love on him as an American family, and keep him confident in the efforts we were making back home.

But even with the good plan and all the re-buying, it all seemed in some way, pouring more salt into larger wounds. We were suffering through a deep gash to the flesh. We felt bled out. This was just first-aid when real surgery was still ahead.

His new school in Uganda was a mixed blessing. Educationally, better than what he had left. But as William donned the red, short sleeved button up shirt, made by some local woman with a foot-powered single-needle sewing machine and then the black shorts with a belt Nita felt it was as if he was putting on a prison uniform.

Soon came time for our second goodbye in as many days. I had to turn my back in retreat, vowing to live and fight another day. I was dreading that last look in the rear window of the van, when we would steer out of the alleyway onto the road for drive back to the Entebbe Airport. To the flight with our names on it, save William.

Pressing heavily upon me were the accusing voices blaming me for the failure. I struggled to adjust to that new walk, rather, that maimed limp. But I also had to look into those brown eyes of a hopeful young man who still believed I had the power to keep a promise. One that I wasn't sure if I had anything left to muster.

Nita had her pain to bear too. Piercing, poignant emotions were crashing down on her like tidal wave. I could see she was trying to hold back, be strong for William's sake. She lifted his chin a number of times as the crestfallen young man stubbornly stared at the dust below his feet. Grasping his face in her two hands, to catch again the bonded connection of trust they had when fear was about teeth, she spoke these words through her and William's mutual tears.

"A promise is a promise. David and I will work from this moment on and come back to get you. Please believe that. I need you to believe that we will come for you."

"I believe." he said. "I will wait for you here."

We turned and walked out of the courtyard and back through the wooden gate held on with one hinge. William didn't move. He stood in the same spot, looking toward the ground, lost in the sudden change of circumstances. The red flapping laundry of school uniforms was the first thing to obscure our final views of him, then the children playing closed in around him, then the gate shut.

And just like the fire pit in our backyard, powered by that limited amount of propane to light the way, I swear I heard the flame inside me go *poof.*

We were out of fuel.

It was one of the darkest days of our lives.

SOME SNAPSHOTS ALONG THE WAY.

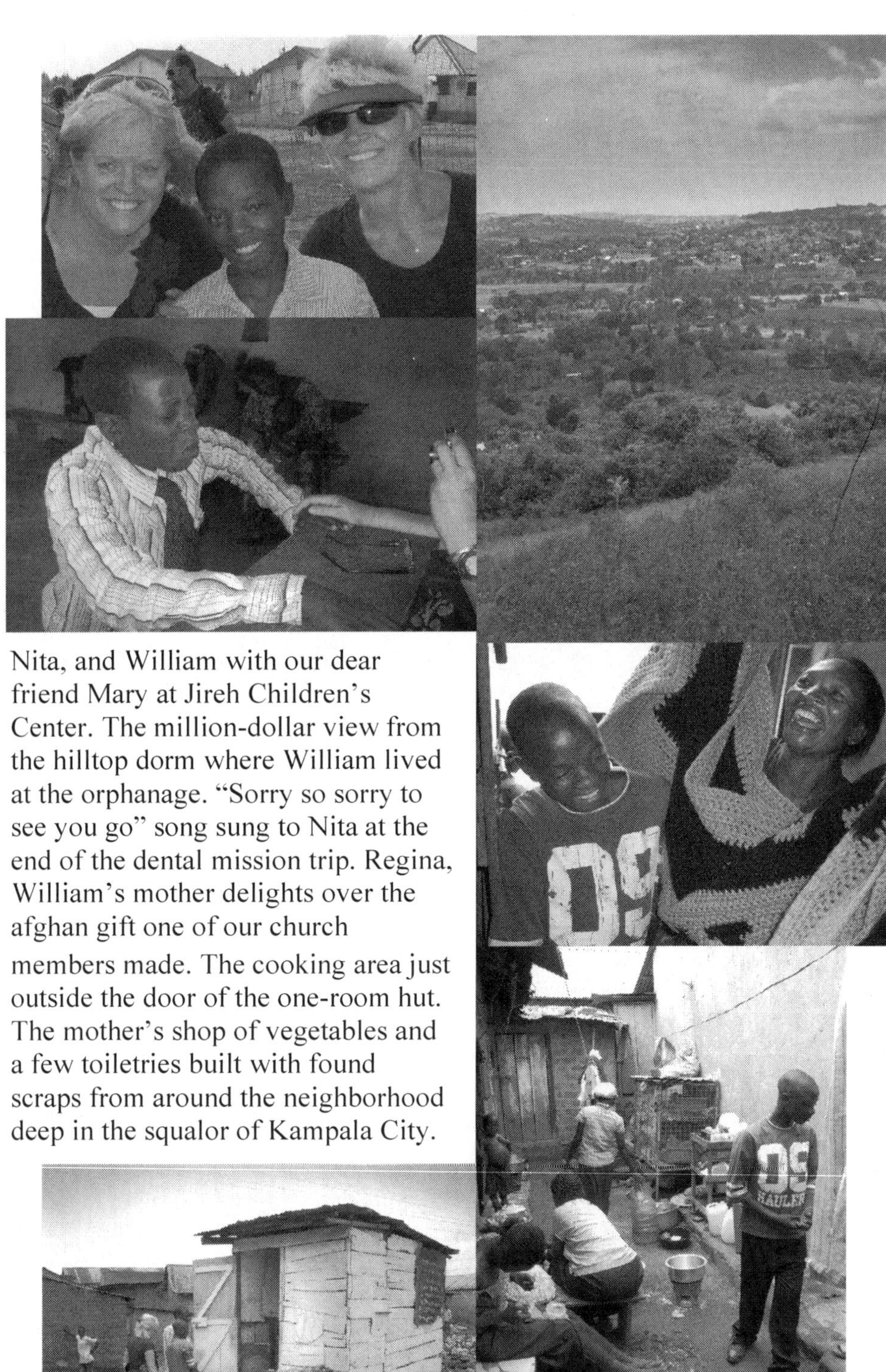

Nita, and William with our dear friend Mary at Jireh Children's Center. The million-dollar view from the hilltop dorm where William lived at the orphanage. "Sorry so sorry to see you go" song sung to Nita at the end of the dental mission trip. Regina, William's mother delights over the afghan gift one of our church members made. The cooking area just outside the door of the one-room hut. The mother's shop of vegetables and a few toiletries built with found scraps from around the neighborhood deep in the squalor of Kampala City.

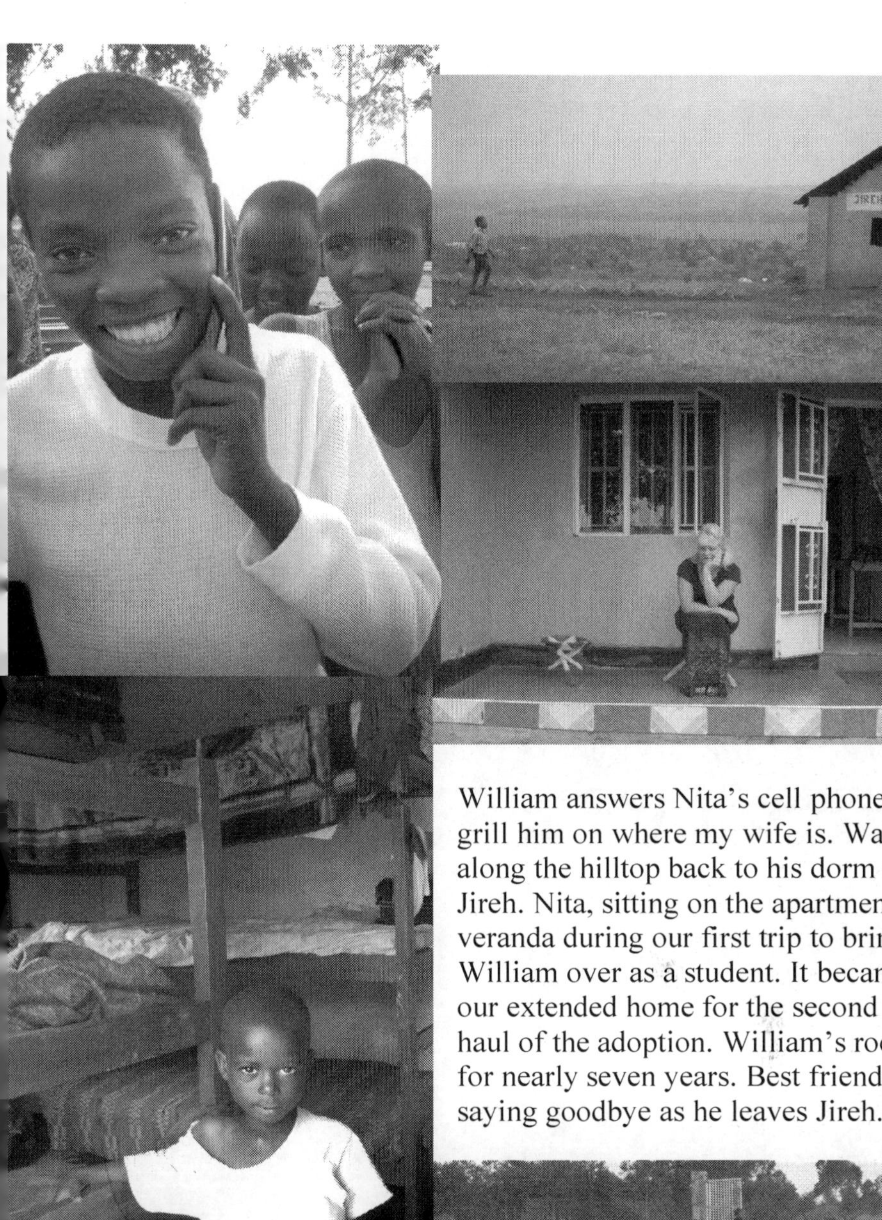

William answers Nita's cell phone as I grill him on where my wife is. Walking along the hilltop back to his dorm at Jireh. Nita, sitting on the apartment veranda during our first trip to bring William over as a student. It became our extended home for the second long haul of the adoption. William's room for nearly seven years. Best friend Paul saying goodbye as he leaves Jireh.

Without the right paperwork to take William to the states as a student, we were forced to leave him behind in a new boarding school. The hardest, tearful goodbye of our lives promising him, "we will fight our hardest and be back as soon as we can". David and Merianne who helped secure William a passport while we were stateside. Legal guardianship hearing in Masaka court on the return trip. A flag waving goodbye to the Visa office and a certain plane ride home…only to be denied returning a day later to start the lengthy adoption process because I said I wouldn't leave without him.

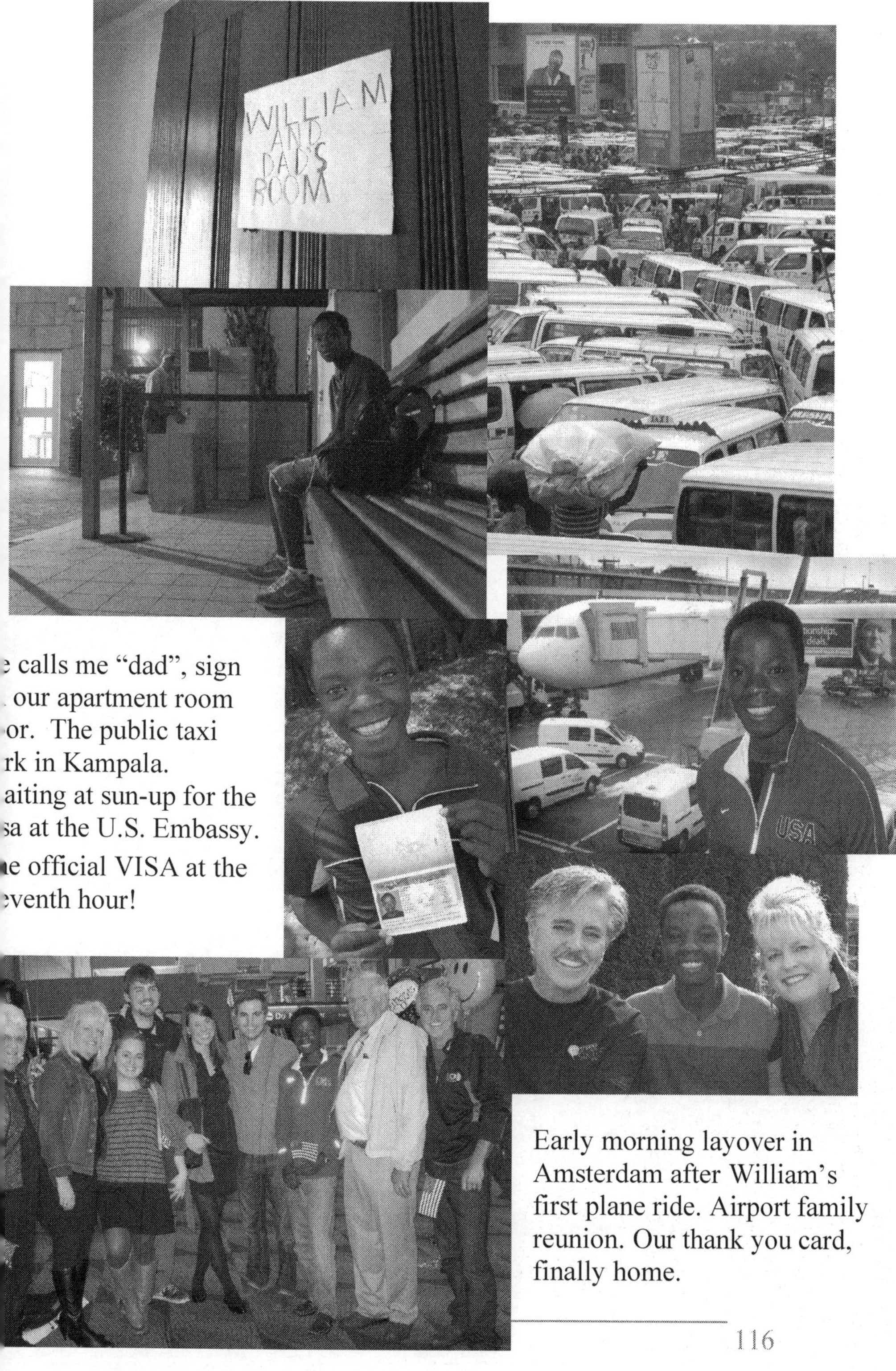

e calls me "dad", sign
our apartment room
or. The public taxi
rk in Kampala.
aiting at sun-up for the
sa at the U.S. Embassy.
e official VISA at the
eventh hour!

Early morning layover in Amsterdam after William's first plane ride. Airport family reunion. Our thank you card, finally home.

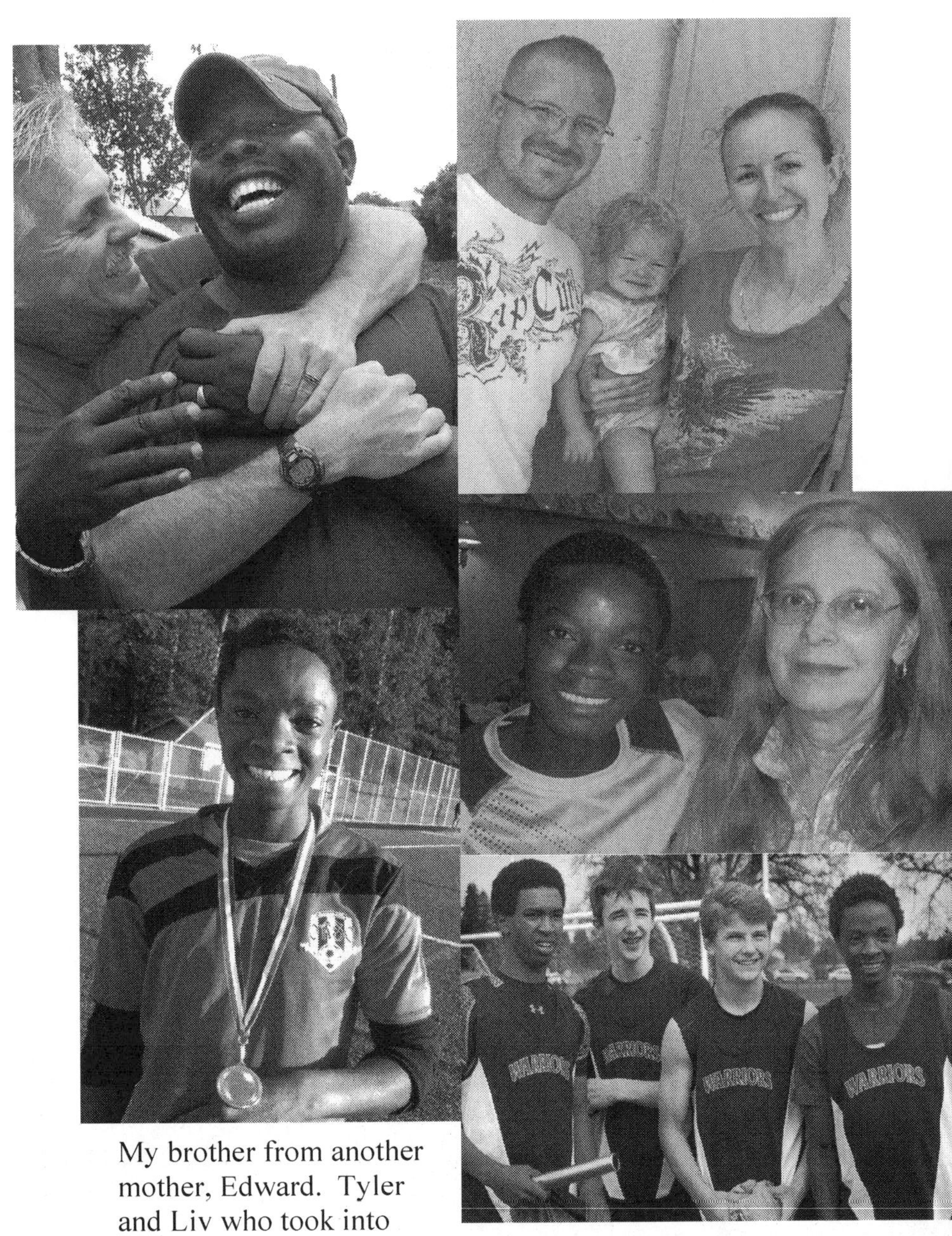

My brother from another mother, Edward. Tyler and Liv who took into their Okoa Refuge, Derek and Peace. Bev who was instrumental in getting our home study paperwork together. William's first middle-school soccer season won the league championship, and the 400 relay team set a school record.

Point man for his eighth grade basketball was his first attempt at hoops, they were league champs. He quickly adopted all things brand name, even down to his socks. The vision came to pass. William's first day at high school in America. I had to snap this quick as not to embarrass him. He made the varsity soccer and track team as a Freshman. The Iphone is still on the list.

13

SHARING THE BURDEN

Nita cried, sniveled and openly wept for the whole thirty-hour trip back home to Oregon.

There was no masking the pain for her, so I figured we might as well wear our true faces for everyone to see, and if so moved, to allow them to join in the burden.

Yet to help mask this impending entourage at our emotional coming home, Garrett, who was picking us up at the airport that Sunday afternoon, called off anyone who wanted drive up to Portland and greet us. It was a relief to know we wouldn't have to face a lot of awkward pity and Christian-eze condolences. Not to mention trying to make others feel better about feeling bad for us.

Maybe that's the problem with masks and not sharing burdens. Masks block the infection we feel we're spreading, but in reality, the mask keeps the needed doses of healing from coming in. By dropping the masks, we may in fact, give some grace to those who are trying to pass on a little blessing. Maybe that's another lesson we still had to learn in the whole process.

The instant we left the airport for the 100-mile jaunt home, I was on my cell phone to get the ball rolling on a home study we needed as part of gaining legal guardianship. I wanted to shave off as much time as I could.

Where and whom to start with was a complete mystery, but I remembered our worship leader had a friend who had adopted four or five special needs kids from the Ukraine. If anyone had a name it would be him. He had a name, Bev, a tenderhearted Christian woman whose calling was helping couples with foreign children. She was in a town just an hour north of us. I left her a message.

Next I called United Airlines and discovered I had enough airline miles to get two tickets. One round trip for me, and a one-way back for William. At first I thought Nita would want to go back, finish what she started, but Nita was always thinking it was going to be me.

It was early fall, my favorite time of year. As we drove south back to Eugene I felt a little warmth from the I Oregon leaves turning the saturated colors of orange, red and yellow. Usually my spirits are more upbeat during this season as I see the change of seasons and God's handiwork. But there was a cloudy sense of urgency about both of us that shrouded the appreciation that particular fall.

By the time we landed, school had already started and October was fast approaching. We spent nearly three desperate weeks in Uganda and now were having to readjust our timeline of when William would start the eighth grade. The wisdom was still to give him a full year in middle school before dropping him into the peer-driven cesspool of higher ed.

We were anxiously trying to put him on the same age progression as a "normal" American student, which at his junior year, would put him among other things, driving in stride with everyone else. And not graduating high school as the only near 20-year old, with a mustache and a false reputation for being the kid held back multiple times, God forbid.

We received numerous phone calls from people wanting to be brought up to speed that weekend. We retold the details so many times that it started to strike us that there was room for many warriors in this story, if we allowed them in. Trying to keep people out of the story because we wanted to limit our pain in telling the story, didn't allow what God was doing by bringing more people into the story. That was His plan.

The more we told people about our plight, the more it seemed right and fitting to surrender to this idea. Unmask what would be the urge to hide, not have to be strong all the time. The more who got involved, the more we had praying, bringing in ideas and resources to help. This seemed to be the better way to proceed through these stormy waters.

That first Monday back, we went to the school to get his F-1 student visa updated for a later start date. Before we left that morning, we were invited by the principal into the main middle school classroom to share the story. You could tell by the kids' concerned faces, that they thought these kinds of stories only happen to people on whom God doesn't have his hand. The clean-cut American-pastor-follower-family should somehow be exempt from these kinds of hardships when they are answering a higher calling.

Our older kids' former teacher was in that classroom. He said some wonderful things about both of the kids and, as we were leaving, the principal asked for William's future class to include him in their daily prayers.

Later that day my phone rang with a most peculiar tone, almost like a boxing bell, as if to signal the start of another round. Though we were still reeling from the headache and fog from the recent knock-out punch, this would prove to be the opening comeback climb off the mat.

It was Bev, the home-study lady.

"Mr. Loveall, you know I only do home studies for adoptions," she said. "I want to help out. I can get the home study done you need done for you in five weeks. You have my word."

"Adoption?" I said. "We just want to bring him here to educate him. Is that the same thing?"

Bev was initially concerned. It was unusual to do a lesser version, but we were also including squeaky clean files and fingerprints the state had from us doing prison ministry.

We discussed the checklist we got from the first immigration attorney and she felt confident to proceed on this tack. And we felt confident, too. Looking back, maybe too confident.

She said a sizable packet would be coming in the mail right away. This became the playbook that set in the order the necessary events and paperwork that would get us back to William and in court, more fully prepared. Bev promised to put us on a fast track if we were up for it.

"It's the only thing we are dedicated to do at this time," I assured her. "This will have all of our waking attention."

Like clockwork the next day, the mailman dropped off a large envelope with a laundry list of things to compile. We began with gathering all the e-mail paperwork first, like letters of references from friends and testimonies from our two older kids. It was then onto the banks to get the financial stuff, collect the pay stubs from work verifying that we could support another family member. We had to provide proof of investments, credit history, assets and a few year's back taxes. And much more.

Our ancient, yellowed birth certificates, once we found them in the attic file, didn't have the proper state seal. We had to get re-issued certified birth documents for both of us. We had to have criminal history checks again. (I discovered Nita had been issued a speeding ticket a while back without me knowing it, but that's another story.)

It turned out to be a thorough grilling second only to a CSI interrogation, one I'm sure would have quickly overwhelmed us if we had to find out all the requirements by ourselves. In a quick couple of days, we added some height and weight to our skinny court file. We were getting even more supporting documents than what the "foul one," back in Uganda, had requested. We were pursuing the sure-fire decision. Trying to plug every possible challenge that might get thrown back at us.

We had also been in regular contact with attorney Justin, who was filing more family documents from Regina's tribe. According to Justin, the judge said he would be available anytime we could make flight arrangements, even if we needed a date near Christmas. By getting a ruling by then, we figured William could still plug into the second half of eighth grade after the holiday break, giving him enough middle school experiences and transition before his freshman year.

Moving down the check-list, we finally came to the installation of the new CO2 and fire smoke detectors, and the emergency home-escape plan. While I was still at the home improvement store, Nita called Bev to make an appointment. I don't even think I got the screwdrivers put away from installing the detectors before she showed up. We'd only been back from Africa three weeks.

The day she was due to arrive, both of us awoke early and made sure the house was cleaner than usual that Friday. At the time, our son Garrett was living with us in transition from finishing college. As part of the home study and because he was under the roof at the time, he was required to be included in the evaluation and interviews and background checks.

Bev arrived and Garrett was the first to be called into the living room. He was, in fact, the one who spent the longest time with her. He's still amused when he remembers the conversation. He said Bev asked him just one question, "If he thought the idea was sound." After he answered yes, Bev talked at length about how unique her job was, what she had seen, and how quickly she gets a feeling for a particular client. Clearly, she knew her stuff. "We talked about everything else but what I thought we were going to," Garrett said.

Because Bev had seen so many homes and complicated situations, I was confident she had her red flags covered the first few minutes she arrived. Yet the best part of the interview was revealed in the few minutes before she left.

"I want to pray for you people and this process," she said. With that, she grabbed both our hands and we formed a small circle in the front room entryway. Bev dove right into the prayerful plea with a spirited Pentecostal pitch. A few moments later, she ended with the "amen" hand squeeze. Nita thanked her and said she was grateful that a covering was put upon the process. We both felt a rush of renewed hope.

Even though we were knocking down some big dominoes, we still didn't have a passport for William. This was a major hurdle heading our Christmas deadline. Because of the shenanigans involving Bob Fitness, the file had been buried deep. According to Justin, the passport, was still "under review."

One of the ideas we had discussed was the possibility of William applying on his own as a regular citizen of Uganda—perhaps with his mother's verification, who lived close to the office. That process, we were told, typically takes a few weeks and wouldn't raise any eyebrows regarding his past connections to us.

The couple we had met in Kampala, shirt-tale relatives to the pastor, David and Merianne, offered to step in and assist. Coincidentally, they had a friend who had a friend who worked at the passport office

We wired them five-hundred thousand schillings, and David put in motion the "Ugandan way" of getting stuff done, which meant that certain people got a few schillings folded into handshakes for some extra attention to the new file as it made its way through the red tape. At one point, David told us during a SKYPE update that the last man in the process needed "just a little more money" and the passport would be in his hands within hours.

Nita, on her way out the door to work that morning, overhead the request and nearly turned her dental scrubs inside out as she jumped into the camera's view.

"You tell whomever you are dealing with that he is not getting another dime out of me until you have the passport in your hands!" she said, pointing a finger at the green computer light.

The next day, David sent us a text saying he had the passport in his hand and asked if it would be OK now with Ms. Nita if he gave the man the money we promised. He seemed a little gun shy after the last SKYPE session, but I had to laugh.

"Give him the rest of the money and tell him 'thank you' for a promise kept," I said.

October raced into November. While glancing over my e-mail junk folder, I realized there was a lost e-mail from Justin buried in under the mortgage ads and personal enhancement temptations.

The title read "have court date."

Justin had secured a court date for December 6, just two days after I scheduled my arrival. The date worked perfectly with our desire for getting William back in time for school right after the holiday break. I immediately called Bev, who assured us the home study would be ready to deliver right before Thanksgiving. So the question was, could I get a frequent flier ticket with less than a 30-day notice with the minimum miles for a round trip for me and one-way back for William? I spoke out a "please Lord" prayer at the same time I pressed out the 800 number on my I-phone.

My first connection to United Airlines' frequent flier number was to a guy named "George." He spoke broken Hindu and sounded like he was a trainee with limited keystroke skills speaking through cardboard tube. So forgive me, I hung up on him.

I instantly hit redial and got connected to a woman with a Midwest drawl from Chicago. I knew this because the first questioned I peppered her with was, "Excuse me, I hate to be rude, but are you from America and habla el English?"

"I am from the great town of Chicago," she said. "Born and raised. English is my first language." By her tone I could tell she was obviously amused. "Now how can I help you, sir?"

I gave her our story's elevator version. She tapped and crackled her keyboard. At the end of my tale, she said she had pulled some kind of magic out of her ticket terminal.

"Oh look, I just found that there are two seats for those exact dates you need. I just booked them for you."

I'm sure, based on the amount of her feverish typing, that she basically hacked those two seats out of thin air or maybe even stole them from the previous customer who didn't have as good a sob story. But also I believe it was because she had a believing heart as well. We didn't talk about God and church, but then again, we didn't have to.

Once again, I felt the sharing of burdens allowed someone else to bless another in the process. Namely, me and Nita.

Our weekly Skyping with William was helping build trust and got all of us over those tough goodbye emotions. At first, he looked tired and stressed from the rigors of the boarding school adjustment. But he was also grateful for the extra sleep he was getting on the weekends at Brian and Angela's place. Our progress kept his hopes alive. Based on the chain of events unfolding, it was looking pretty certain that William would be spending Christmas in the states with us.

The internet on those Saturdays was intermittent. We'd connect and quickly say something then "image freeze." Being routinely cut short in the middle of a story was frustrating, especially when we were limited to once-a-week contact, but when Uganda schools began their two-month holiday break, we spoke more often.

By early November, William was living with our friends full time and rapidly becoming westernized under their roof. He was wearing clothes belonging to their son, learning to play hide and seek, and looking wide-eyed about the anticipation of his first American Thanksgiving.

It was a rainy Saturday morning, November 24. In only eight days the plane back to Uganda was leaving with me on it. I was checking e-mail just after my Saturday long run. Ever since the October jet lag had faded, I had been working out like a man possessed. It was as if something was chasing me, as if there was something ahead I needed to be prepared for. For weeks, each of my runs was timed. Never satisfied, I would push a little harder, add more sit-ups, and crank out chin ups until I couldn't do another. There was a fight to be had, and my gut was preparing for battle. Another loss wasn't an option. I could feel that deeper than ever.

Still in her pajamas, Nita was in the other room watching the TV morning news while I downed the last of my coffee and banana protein smoothie. Scanning down my e-mail messages, I saw a message from Justin, sent late the previous Friday evening. In the title line, in had all capital letters, were the words, "DO NOT COME! PLEASE NOT NOW."

My spirit sank to that familiar place I had thought was left behind, back to that gut-wrenching, uncontrollable defeat when we left William in the school courtyard. With cautious angst I opened the e-mail hoping in part, that it would be a veiled virus from someone wanting to scam my password and bank information, but it was not. It was from Justin, who was telling us that the bottom had fallen out again.

It was brief, pieced together in broken grammar, which was typical of Justin, so I held out hope that it could still be some e-mail hacker. Until I got past the title and the traditional Ugandan intro.

"Greetings, I hope this finds you well in the Lord," it read. "Please do not come. The judge has gone on vacation and will not return to court until after the new year. Contact me then and we will see what we can do. Please do not come now."

Whirling to find my cell phone, I checked the time difference, 5 p.m. their time. I dialed Justin while telling Nita, "We have a problem."

Justin said hello. "Sorry Justin I must cut to the point," I said. "Is there any way we can change the location of the hearing? I mean do we have to use this judge? Can we possibly change the court to Masaka town and present it in front of a local magistrate where William is living?"

I wasn't about to panic or cancel those miracle airline tickets, but even this idea, was a long shot.

"Mmmmm, mmmm," he said, which is Ugandan for "Gee, this plan just might work."

"I suppose we could look into refiling in another district. We only have a week, but I will text you with any news by tomorrow. You had better start praying."

"Justin!" I said. "When do you think we've stopped?"

We prayed and paid—this time 500,000 more schillings ($175 US) to allow Justin to file the documents

We arrived at the Eugene Airport. It was like a movie moment from *Castaway* where the character played by Tom Hanks kisses his girl goodbye and turns to board the FedEx plane that later crashes, leaving him stranded for four years on a deserted island. I said virtually the same thing.

I kissed Nita goodbye at the airport, went through security and turned back.

"I promise the Christmas lights will get hung the day I return, with plenty of time before the big day," I said, blowing her another "I'll-be-right-back-with-the-package" kiss. Under my breath I whispered these words which only caught the attention of the TSA agent: "And I won't come back empty-handed. I won't fail you this time."

I waved through the window once I got my shoes and belt back on. She was wearing an anxious face hidden by an artificial smile. In my carryon pack was a green expansion file a few inches thick. Certified copies of everything six deep, including a half-dozen notarized copies of my passport.

I was trying the best I could to wear a convincing mask that everything would work out—even if, behind the mask, I wasn't completely sure.

and cover the expenses of sending one of his aids in a taxi three hours away to Masaka town.

By the end of the day, I put a post on Facebook with a photo of William and me from the previous trip taken on the porch of the apartment in Brian and Angela's compound. My arm was around him. His bald head hit me at my shoulders. Both of us are wearing black Three Sixteen Ministries shirts, smiling. A salt-and-pepper image, either meant to be tied at the hip, or at least destined to share each other's laundry.

The dire post read "NEED PRAYER FRIENDS!" with details of the latest twist in our story.

Many people, including those outside our immediate circle got on board, commented and hit the 'like' button. The story of William had struck a chord in many people on the fringes. Its made-for-TV details was moving and stretching the boundaries of many people's faith, just as it was stretching ours.

The next time on Skype we told Brian and Angela the news. William and their son Morgan were outside working on a fort to play their next round of live-fire air soft wars. We called William to the computer and briefed him of the change—again. He said that for the last few weeks, he had been fasting for the judge, "the foul one" but would change his focus. A prayer fast shift. No worries. Whatever.

On Monday, Justin called. "David, you may not believe this, but I have found a judge in Masaka who will hear our case," he said. "And we have a court date."

"Yeeees!!!" I yelped in celebration. "When is the court date?"

"December seventh. This means you can come now, so will you be here by then?"

"I will be there with two days to spare," I said, nearly in tears.

Thanksgiving that year, by the very definition, was one of real thanks for us. We Skyped William once we put our turkey in the oven and asked him how his first "American" celebration was. Apparently, it was a town event for all the out-of-country Muzungu's missionaries. Fifty people were at his host's house.

"My most favorite part of the Thanksgiving meal today was the whipping cream," he said. I couldn't tell by the pixilated image, but I swear he still had some stuck to his face.

My flight was set to leave in the afternoon right after I preached Sunday morning, December 2. I packed light. Nita wasn't even counting this as a real trip, just a short jaunt long enough to get in and get William out.

One of the last things I did before leaving was to tape a "fire evacuation" plan drawing on William's bedroom door. The graph paper and colored markers map of how to get down the stairs and out the front door. It looked like a project I dug out of the saved memory box papers from the third grade. It was the very last required detail of the home study and the final preparation to his arrival. We had an American and Ugandan flag hung over his bed.

One of the closing scriptures that Sunday was taken from Luke 14:33 in *The Message*, "Simply put, if you're not willing to take what is dearest to you, whether plans or people, and kiss it good-bye, you can't be my disciple. This means you."

I said that while pointing to the congregation. But you know what they say, "One finger pointing away, four fingers pointing back at you."

At the close of service, the Three Sixteen church family gathered around Nita and me to pray for court success, blessings, and safe return back with William.

14

LEGAL GUARDIAN

In preparing for the trip, I had made several outspoken declarations on my morning warrior runs. Some of the folks along the route started keeping their blinds shut when I would go by, crazy runner in the hood.

I could feel the enemy trying to thwart this calling. I continued to shout proclamations on the summits of my hilly runs. One pledge is that when my feet landed on Ugandan soil, I would stick two spirit swords in the ground, proclaim victory to the battle ahead. The kind of stuff real battle howling heroes do.

When I landed and was on the Ugandan asphalt, I repeated the mantra.

"It's time to stick these swords right here," I said to nobody but myself. I grabbed the sky with my left hand and thrust it once down towards the ground. "Lord, this is the sword of truth. This is your word, your power. I place this sword here to lead and to fight ahead of whatever opposes me."

Switching my carry-on pack to the other side, I grabbed the sky again and with my right hand and thrust spiritually through the hardened blacktop.

"Lord, this is the other sword. The one you said was enough when Peter in the garden said they had two. This is the sword of warriorship. The one I vow to pick up every moment and to fight with. The sword I will yield with power and force that you have been training for me these past months. My prayer is that it is swift and strong, and sheathed at my side a week from Saturday, when William and I board our plane, right here, to come home. In Jesus' name."

So much for warriorship; one of my two suitcases wasn't on the carousel. Welcome to Uganda. I spotted a woman near the customs desk who routinely works with the US2UGANDA4LIFE mission people. She helped me file a quick missing bag report ahead of the line and then wheeled my cart for me through the exit without even a look from the other customs officers.

"Mr. David it was great seeing you again!" she said. I pray your journey here will be a success and that your bag is found by tomorrow."

I had hoped so, because the missing bag was the one with Angela's birthday gifts and decorations from Nita. Didn't want those to miss the big bash.

"Great prayer!" I yelled back to the customs lady. "I am believing with you!"

Through the small crowd of people holding signs with names of tourist groups on them, I spotted a white man coming toward me who looked just like Jesus. Literally. It was Brian with William, who zoomed toward me like a Pro Bowl cornerback, then hugged me deeply.

I grabbed his boyish brown face in my hands and made him look at me, locking my eyes to his.

"This time, this trip," I said. "I am not leaving with out you, I promise you that."

"I know that, Dad," he said.

Wait, did he just say "Dad?" Before that could really sink in, I was swallowed up in a group hug with Brian and Angela. We hurriedly zipped through the waiting taxi drivers and within a few minutes we were in the back of their silver mini-van. It was surreal to be back in the equatorial enigma of Uganda, mindlessly catching up on the crazy events of the past weeks and heading down the same two-lane road back to Masaka. Major deja vu'.

Brian volunteered to pick everyone up, including Regina and the uncle, the day of court on Friday morning in his van. He knew exactly what the formula was to get us to the venue on time. On his advice, we agreed to tell everyone court was an hour sooner than it was, hoping to get a leg up on the "Ugandan time." We couldn't be late or we'd be left off the docket as a no show. As it was, the extra time helped us track down the uncle who we finally found sitting in a darkened corner of the dining area when we couldn't get him to answer our pounding on his room door.

We were the first ones to arrive. Justin went right to work. He gathered us around a greeting kiosk counter (the daily greeter hadn't even arrived yet). He wiped the dust off with his suit sleeve and broke out some last-minute papers needing some official stamps before the judge could take them into the case file.

In the courtyard behind the entrance was a group of offices, each with stacks of files against the walls, and a few city workers acting like they were having a coffee break in each closet-sized room. Except there was no coffee. The only refreshments came from the wandering guy with the bowl of g-nuts wrapped in cellophane. It had all the feel of casual Friday. Nobody in a big hurry, no work really being done at the moment, just a few awkward curious stares my direction which was becoming a daily occurrence for this particular Muzungu.

A few hours went by. I paced inside, then out. I sat on the steps with the locals, leaned against the wall in the sliver of shade from the rising temperature, counted the decorative holes in the brick wall separating the entry room from the front door. I went up the stairs to the second floor a few times to see if there was any activity in the ghostly, wooden adorned courtroom.

I meandered back down to the ground floor, counting the steps out of sheer boredom again but this time there was a young woman clerk, looking similar to perfume lady of the Kampala court but not as fragrant, talking to Justin. It was nearly 11am. We'd been there already three hours.

"It's time." Justin said. "The judge is ready to see us."

Bouncing quickly back up the stairs, the uncle, William, Regina with the baby in tow, and I dashed through the vintage courtroom and out a side door to a balcony—where we waited for another half an hour outside of the judge's private office.

The door squeaked open to the tiny office where the smartly dressed assistant waved us in. Once inside we greeted the female judge, who barely looked at us and didn't smile. She cracked the file in front of her, firing questions to Justin and to the uncle. She spoke strictly Lugandan, and sternly.

The home study surfaced in the subsequent page-turning and the questions started being leveled at me. In harsh English.

Why do you want this child? How will you raise him? Where will he go to school? Do you have enough money? Where is your wife?

It seemed the "foul one" disease had come to the smaller courts a hundred miles away, but I wasn't about to make waves. She asked her questions again without looking up, without reacting to my answers, and without any expression whatsoever. That is until she went back to questioning Regina, who was holding her now four-month-old baby.

"That there is your baby?" the judge said.

Regina nodded.

"Here you are, sitting in front of me, so that someone can take responsibility of your first-born son because you can't look after him, and you bring in here another baby?" The judge wedged her glasses back onto the front of her nose and then leveled more distain to William's birth mother in Lugandan.

"What's it going to be in a few years? Will you be bringing back this small child back into my court to find another one to take it as well? You need to be responsible and take care of what you've brought into this world."

Her cantankerous cross-examination seemed personal, like she was fed up with Muzungu's taking her own children out of her country. I instantly started to worry, especially when she hastily shut the file and stood up without finishing her last thought.

"I will give you my ruling in a few days. Good day." With that dismissal, she exited out the door behind her desk, and never looked back, leaving all of us slightly aghast.

"That went very well," Justin said. "She has no choice but to grant us the legal guardianship. The proper papers are filed, and the fact that we have proved William is an orphan, and his family can't—and won't—care for him. Trust me David, you will be awarded his guardian."

I'm sure my puzzled "must-have-missed-something" look is what prompted the next comment. "Don't worry this time David, it's our turn to win this time."

Nobody else seemed as enthused, but I trusted him. If he thought it went well, then I was going to think the same.

"I don't think that was a really good meeting," William said as we walked out the gate to the road, "but everything seems OK inside me. This will prove to be a very good day."

He buried his buzz cut under my arms, we grinned. Good day, I suspect, was because I was back in the country like I said I would be, and mine, because I felt the second to last domino had fallen. The legal game was just about over.

Facebook lit up over the weekend. Our prayer requests were shared and commented on numerous times. People were praising and confident William's arrival was imminent for Christmas.

Sunday, we went to church with Brian and Angela, where we met and told the story to a dozen other Muzungu missionaries. They all were noticeably moved by the obvious hand of God. Afterward, I played my first game of cricket, a nice diversion from wondering about the pending decision.

Monday morning I reconnected with Pastor Edward Mbuyi. We met for an early morning Bible journaling session at the apartment and I gave him is own, dri-fit Nike, Three Sixteen Ministries shirt. He's got a heart the size of Texas and his words are always well seasoned, like a great meat rub. When they meet you, they always rub you the right way and sink in.

"David, I want to tell you when you were here last and I came to the men's conference, I want to say that you changed my life, brother." Edward looked me right between the eyes and patted his chest, the one that now sported the logo of our startup church across it.

"Those two pillars you taught, 'speak the truth always, and do what you say,' has made me into a better man of God. I can now stand before God confidently knowing now that I am in the right place. I am in the place of being a father, and being a man serving Him, instead of running from God. I owe that to you, my brother."

We bear-hugged in mutual appreciation. His head paused momentarily over my shoulder and he spoke right into my ear.

"Uganda is calling you my friend. You will be a man who changes the men of this country." His prophetic words were deep, like the actor who does the Lion King voice. And they petrified me. In my mind, Uganda was a soon-to-be memory, starting Saturday, upon our midnight take-off. And here he was, suddenly introducing a whole new possibility.

Justin and I mobile-messaged each other off and on until late Monday morning. His last text read that he anticipated a response by that afternoon. I was way past pins and needles; more like hot coals. Around 2:45 p.m., my phone went off with Justin's name across the caller I.D.

"David, the judge has ruled in our favor. We have the legal guardianship!"

For him, it was proof of his integrity and diligence in the kind of case he had limited experience with. For me, it was like the key block in a football game that set up the next play to score. In any case, we had our answer and our long-awaited celebration ensued.

"We are now William's legal guardians!" I shouted outside our apartment and then over my mobile phone in an immediate call to Nita. The midnight time difference broke her out of a sound sleep and she screamed so loud I'm sure the neighbors heard the entire conversation.

"The papers will be picked up tomorrow and we should be on our way back to Kampala to get his passport stamped on Friday. What a great Christmas this is going to be!"

I had been in contact multiple times with the Kampala visa office since Friday, phone-tagging my way through the red tape. The office confirmed the F-1 papers were uploaded, the online applications were in the computer system and all they needed was to see the official court order.

With Christmas fast approaching, Nita reminded William and me that the Christmas lights hadn't been hung yet. She said she was going to have us men do it when we arrived home in a few days.

Justin sent his well-versed junior associate back to Masaka that Tuesday morning to do the final acceptance of the guardianship. When he arrived, I took a "selfie" picture of the three of us in the vacant courtroom as he was making sure the final papers were exactly in order. He advised me to get six more copies of the court order making sure the official stamp and judge's signature was on each of them, just as a precaution.

"You never know when you're going to need them," the young attorney advised with sage-like wisdom.

When the sharply adorned woman assistant to the judge handed me the papers in a large envelope, I asked her politely if I could have a few more copies, and passed them back to her with 20,000 schillings on top of it.

"I will get right on that sir," she said with a smile. "My name is Sharon. I will personally see to this. It won't take but a little while to get this done."

Perhaps that 20,000 schillings got her to move quickly, but the subsequent people down the ladder who actually made the copies, were a few schillings slower. It took 90 minutes for them to make six copies.

Never mind, on Thursday we headed from Masaka to Kampala to get the visas—in style. I had hired Peter, a driver friend of Brian and Angela's whose air-conditioned Mercedes fit our upbeat moods.

When getting into the car, Angela screamed and darted back into the house, saying something about forgetting a gift for William. She reappeared out from under the porch shade waving an American flag in circles above her head, like she was cheering at a space shuttle landing.

"When you land in America and you get off that plane, you wear this!" Her giddy energy danced around

William as she wrapped him in Old Glory, capping the boogie with a big ol' southern drawl kiss on his cheeks.

"Thank you, thank you very much," William said. "And thank you for caring for me until, um, Dad got here."

His voice broke down, and he stammered to finish his statement, overcome with emotion. He had been part of a real family for over a month. They had loved him like he hadn't been for his entire life. I misted up as well, grateful for their sacrifice and sharing of their family while we faced numerous crises back home.

The pullout from Uganda seemed complete and nearly done. William was mine now, legit and legal and now tied to a western family for the foreseeable future.

We were just a stamp away from getting back before Christmas, and pulling up those fighting swords I left stuck in the airport tarmac.

15

DAD

Batman was my hero.

He battled against evil old school—fists, words, strategy, teamwork, gadgets, a little luck and the belief that good guys always win. Sounded like the perfect dad to me. When came down to it, the super-saving ingredient in being a hero isn't in the cape or the gadgets, but in the decision to lay down one's self for another. At the end of the episode, that's what makes a hero a real hero. That's what makes a dad, a dad.

As we pulled onto the Kampala Rwanda Highway and headed east along Lake Victoria, I was soaking it all in, knowing these might be my last memories of Uganda.

William was mostly quiet, but was engaged with Peter as our young driver questioned him on what he was going to do once he got to America. Peter encouraged him to keep the upright character qualities he had learned toward adults in his country, and to respect his new parents for what they had done for him.

"You must always remember where you came from," Peter said. "You have a debt to your people to become the great man that God has called you to be."

As he spoke, I drifted away in my own thoughts about great men. Heroes of the faith, men I've known who've done honorable deeds and laid down their lives for promises or noble causes.

A few words from coaches in my past came to me who had said some of the very same life-lesson laws that Peter was laying before William.

I thought of my own dad, who sadly, I rarely speak to anymore—long story—I wondered if he would be proud of what I was doing. Yet all of the day-dream approval-seeking from others wasn't going to compare to my wife's face of unconstrained joy when we got off the airplane in a few days. That would be the greatest validation of this hard-fought battle.

The second traffic circle greeted us with that familiar hazy, reddish, African brown traffic fog from the throng of vehicles. I sneezed a few times, William coughed.

"I do not like Kampala," William said. "I do not feel good when I come here."

We drove past the Embassy, ominously familiar. There were the gun-toting guards at the driveway and up on the dirt mounds, behind them, the impenetrable concrete walls topped with razor wire swirls. The fortress stretched out for a few blocks in either direction of the main entrance. It was against the law to stop in front, so there were always people walking alongside the shoulder-less road, elbow to mirror to all the passing vehicles. On this afternoon, many had handkerchiefs or scarves across their faces to filter out the grime and exhaust.

Up the hill a mile or so was the hotel Brian had recommended. Cheap, clean and breakfast for 40,000 schillings. Add another 10,000 for William and we're only in it about $18 a night. By the time we got to our one-window room, the power went out, of course. Which meant the fan wouldn't work, which meant the hot, city haze settled stagnantly under our mosquito netting over each of the twin beds.

Neither of us slept well. Some of it was the anticipation, most of it was the swelter. We arose early, downed a simple egg and Musliek cereal and walked down the hill to the U.S. Embassy. The sunrise coolness from the passing vehicles was a welcomed treat compared to the unpleasant festering stillness back in the room.

Once our packs passed security, we locked them up in the lockers under the outside waiting area. The person in the window by the secure front door put us in the line for the morning's business of "country relations." I clutched the green file folder under my arm as if it were a football that I didn't dare fumble. It had all of our passport copies, court orders, and home study duplicates. It was our ticket to freedom, or at least the approval of our escape plan.

The door opened promptly at 8:30 a.m. and we were the third party through. We walked through the manicured courtyard, up the steps to another waiting room that had three interview closets. No chairs.

One of the clerks called William and I to be in the first interview closet within a few minutes of being seated. We squeezed inside and closed the door behind us, facing a woman who already had a thin file in her hands. We slid the Legal Guardianship, the court order and modified home study through the tray and answered some basic questions.

After briefly getting what she needed from me, she turned to William and asked him to raise his right hand to take an oath. She told him that if he swore to tell the truth, even if the truth prevented him from leaving the country, he needed to stick to that truth. He gulped nervously, and I winked in his direction.

"It's all good," I said. "She just needs to hear you say that you know what's going on."

The first question was if he wanted to go with me to America and why. I don't think I'd ever heard him say why he wanted to go, and I wasn't sure if telling this clerk about his vision from God would put a "crazy" stamp across our file. But as any 14-year-old kid would answer some squirming questions from an adult behind bulletproof glass, I believe he did well enough to satisfy the official.

"I am going to America for my education," he said. His brevity I'm sure prompted the next question.

"And do you want to go with this man here making this decision under your own free will?" the official said.

"Yes, yes, I do. I believe this is what's best for me."

We were told to go to the outside waiting area while she got the guy who does the Visas. An American-looking woman was waiting her turn there as well.

"Come here often?" I joked.

"I've been here two months. Yeah, I come here way too often." Now that my blinders were off, she did look a little frazzled.

"What's the deal with that?"

It turned out to be another painstakingly complicated story about adoption gone sideways. This, confusingly from a system that claims to want to do good by the nation's children. She said her husband had been back in America for the past month while she stayed behind to finish up a the last of the red tape. This particular morning, she was seeking medical-exam permission to take her new baby to state-sponsored clinic so she could be cleared to go to the U.S.

"You know all kids that are brought into the U.S. from Uganda have to go through this medical thing. It takes like two weeks and costs nearly $500."

An unexpected knot started to form in my gut.

It had now been over an hour since we were in the closet with the green glass. The sun was heating up the shade and I had already made a couple of trips to the bathroom to splash some water on my face. When I got back the second time, the American woman had left.

"Hey William, where did the woman go?"

"I don't know dad, but she came out of the room with the same woman we saw, and she was crying."

My spontaneous prayer was cut short by the guard at the door. "You two are next," he said nonchalantly opening the door.

"Room three this time," he said.

I hadn't seen anyone go into room number three all morning. This must be a good sign.

An American-looking woman with fair hair in her mid-thirties greeted us and asked us to be seated. Her introduction was a string of supervisory tags; basically she was the big cheese of this section of the U.S. Embassy.

As the papers in front of her were spread out, William's brand new passport peeked out from the bottom of the pile. She patted the top of the stack and leaned into the window. I awaited for her rubber-stamped approval.

"I'm afraid I can't."

"Excuse me, sorry to interrupt," I broke in. "Are you the supervisor, or should we be speaking to someone else?"

"I am the person who decides what happens here."

Instantly, I gathered my groveling humility and apologized for interrupting, buttoned my lip, and leaned intently into the tinted glass, catching the hint of her irritation.

"After looking over your file and what you want to do with William, I'm afraid you don't have the right visa for him to gain entry into the United States."

Flabbergasted, I fired back the chain of events with the judge and what he led us to believe we needed. We had thickened the file, satisfied the Ugandan demands, come back and got the guardianship and court orders. We paid for the visa online and had a receipt.

"Everything is proper and done according to their laws" I said.

"That may well be the case, but the United States has requirements you have to meet so they will allow him into the country. You haven't done all of that."

William was frozen as he heard the words of denial. A couple of tears slid down his stunned face.

Fight mode kicked in, and I piled back through the glass every shred of evidence, and advice from lawyers. I even laid a heavy a story or two of guilt, expenses and pain on her. It was as if I was talking to a statue. And it wasn't lady liberty.

"I'm really sorry," she said. "The real problem is, by proving you had qualifications to gain legal guardianship, you proved William has no family connection here in this country. If in fact, I could give you a visa to bring him into the United States as a student, once he got out of school, he would have no ties back here that would require him to return. This is why the U.S. will not let him enter. He's got to be connected to a family."

The heaving pressure in my chest released as I slumped into the chair in utter disbelief. I rubbed my forehead like a genie lamp trying wish up a miracle, but to no avail. William's steady tears were dripping onto his shirt and both forearms bore the wet wipes of pain from his runny nose.

Knowing the hurt and distress Nita was going to feel, I riled up with a final dose of fury, tapping on the glass and raising my voice to a more serious level.

"Why are you doing this?" I said. "You have the power to make this happen. I'm sure you understand, we're the good guys! We're the ones taking this kid to a better place. We've done what was asked us to do. Now, damn it, give us the damn visa! You have enough to make the decision to know that this is the right thing for you to do here, now why can't you do the right thing?"

"Look Mr. Loveall, I have laws and procedures to follow dictated by the Homeland Security and the United

States government. According to those, you do not have what you need to bring William into the states. I'm sorry for the situation you find yourself in. Surely you're right, I could let you leave the country with him, but you would be stopped at our borders and sent back here."

I'd already crossed a line with my attack. The only thing left was an attempt at mercy.

"Well then what the hell am I supposed to do now?" I said.

"You can leave William here and come back with the proper paperwork. It will need to be the proper adoption paperwork because contrary to what you heard, you cannot take a minor out of a country on a student visa and then maybe decide to adopt them later."

I was crumbling at an exponential rate, my mind spinning so fast and spiraling out of control.

"Here is a list of what you will have to do. There are ten very specific things you must have to gain a visa for a minor child, Mr. Loveall. Mr. Loveall, are you still with me?"

Unconsciously at some point I had grabbed William's hand, not necessarily for his support, but for mine.

She went over the ten adoption items at least three times. I couldn't comprehend a one, my mind elsewhere. William began to openly weep.

The woman slid the file with the unstamped passport on top of it under the glass.

"If you can get right on this, Mr. Loveall, you could have all the work done within six months or sooner," she said.

"What—? What am—? How—?"

She leaned down to the tray.

"You know you could put William back in a boarding school in Masaka and return in time to catch your flight. Mr. Loveall, I recommend you do that and when the paperwork is done in the U.S., come see me and I will personally make sure you get the visa."

"I can't do that. I can't leave without him. I promised."

The woman curtly left the window. I turned and, with William, walked out. The exit turnstile emptied us both right in front of the lockers where we had locked up our backpacks, but we both kept walking.

"Excuse me sir!" a guard yelled. "You must not forget your things."

It was all I could do to turn around. My legs felt like I had just run a marathon, my chest panting like at summit altitude.

When I tell this part of the story, people will sometimes interrupt me and attest they couldn't imagine fighting this hard to bring someone into their family. But heroics isn't one large jump on a grenade or landing a crucial knock out punch at the right time or even daring death to rescue someone.

It's being Batman. It's knowing that limited humanity mixed with divine bearing is what makes these crucial decisions so important. It reveals one's hidden bravery when there's overpowering pressure to give up. What you decide next, based on what you've promised, is who you become.

This is a moment where heroes are made. At the point when checking out to save your own skin seems like the best idea. And you realize another opportunity awaits. A chance to enter into the honor of knights and the round table. To don a cape, to make a difference in someone else's life.

Yelling through the traffic noise, I put my nose within inches of William's like I did at the airport, clutching his face in my hands, staring right through the doubt.

"William, I promised I wasn't leaving with out you and I meant it!" I shouted. "I don't even know what the next decision is, but I expect the first thing is we gotta' find a place to live. So let's suck it up together and take care of that first. God will do the rest. Are you with me?"

"Yes, Dad." he said.

I turned to march back to the hotel and he shouted to the back of my head.

"I'm glad you're not leaving. I'm glad you're my dad."

16

WHITE FLAG MOMENT

There's a point where God moves a person closer, fully to self-defeat, to re-validate one's faith in Him.

It's solely for your benefit. This movement is to again, show how trustworthy God is. It comes only after you fully surrender. Again.

I call this, "a white flag moment."

At that intersection, it feels the Almighty is saying, "Let's throw everything about your life into a rusty barrel and burn it. When all is gone except that one true seed, that my child, is what we will plant somewhere else, and cultivate together."

Those other seeds are usually the ones we carry around, death-gripped in our hands, unwilling to either let go or let grow. They stay buried, for whatever reason, primarily from fear, which then feeds lack of faith. These moments assess who we are and what kind of trust in God we have. Can I embrace a true "white flag" moment and cast those seeds out of my clutched hand?

In those times, after the seeds are finally cast—or forced—they rarely take root. But you gotta' give 'em all up at once, including that most valuable one you might be saving. If not, then nothing has any chance of taking root. That's full white flag surrender.

That's what it felt like walking back up the hill to the hotel. The hotel where we were supposed to be leaving from the next afternoon for a flight home.

Mincing around in my head was how every part of my life was going to take a major blow, or be wiped out entirely. Before we added on the journey of starting Three Sixteen Church, I had spent 28 years of building a successful freelance photography career. Those regular clients were used to instant service and a smile—the kind that only comes from sacrificing much of my personal schedule to meet their deadlines. My reputation had been to under promise and over deliver. But working from Africa, would be impossible, not to mention a tough commute.

Despite all my loyalty beliefs from years of knowing my business clients and even their kids, I knew that a huge chunk would be forced to move on and not return, succumbing to the old saying, "what you don't feed, dies." I surmised that even to the most long-term and loyal when faced with a nebulous return date, would eventually go to someone else. After all, no one is irreplaceable in this world, especially in the photo biz. Who could blame them?

How about who would step into the shoes to pastor the newly formed and needy church? Who and what and how would that work continue with only 40 to 50 members? People scatter without a constant shepherd. On top of the work worries, Nita would have to handle all the duties of running our personal rental property business which had been in my sole custodianship since I convinced her to let me cash in my meager stock market funds to start the investment venture.

And the most important part: the husband, father, the fulfiller of family responsibilities. Plus my daughter was getting married in the summer. Would I even make it to walk her down the aisle if I had to stay here and slog through an African time frame of red tape?

It was nearly midnight, Nita's time, when I made the phone call with the worst of news.

"Hey babe," my voice trailed off. I could hear her try and answer coherently and quickly, dispensing the fog of sound sleep on her side of the planet.

"I hate to tell you this but it looks like William and I aren't going to be able to come home for a while.

"What?" she said. I could hear the movement of her sitting up hastily from her pillows. "Why? What's going on. What happened?"

"Apparently we've shot ourselves in the foot by believing bad advice by the first immigration lawyer in Eugene, who told us this path was a no-brainer." I said. "Since we've proven William is an orphan, and I now have legal custody of him, the U.S. now won't let him into the country without full immigration status, which we don't have."

"So are you now saying we have to fully adopt him before you can bring him home?"

"Yeah, something like that. I've got a list of ten major hurdles we have to clear before we can get an immigration visa approved. It's the only entry condition he can get as a minor to be allowed into the states."

There was a long pause.

"David, that could take months."

I sighed heavily.

"Yeah I know." I said. "We gotta' start from scratch. We have to start by applying for a whole new type of visa. That can't even happen without a complete adoption home study and immigration packet going through all of the Department of Homeland Security processes. I'm sorry I can't hang the Christmas lights."

With the exception of the list I had in my hand, I didn't even know what to do next. Every step on the list was going to take a specific length of time and the math was adding up. People. Red tape. DHL overnight packages.

Waiting. A flurry of unanswered questions that bounced back and forth between us like an unending volleyball rally getting more intense with each concern.

My first concern was cash flow. If I wasn't shooting pictures, there wasn't going to be money to pay the mortgage. That, I feared, would reek irreparable havoc on our finances. The costs associated to process William's adoption were unknown, but according to the couples we spoke to in the courtrooms, it could be upwards of 20,000. That could wipe us out entirely.

I was thinking the worst. That's how I prepare. I think deep down, both of us knew this was going to be an extended haul, more than just a handful of weeks. This could potentially be our worst nightmare in our 30-plus year marriage.

Nita's health-care worker qualms weighed in with other worries. "How much insulin and supplies do you have?"

I wasn't even thinking about that. Being a type 1 diabetic if I eat without injecting, my blood sugar can climb to dangerously high levels which complicates my health greatly. It nearly takes a math degree to balance the ratio of insulin-to-food intake an equation that gets even more complicated when figuring in foreign cuisine. This would be a complete re-programming of my routine being in Africa for an extended time frame, especially without the necessary supplies. It's an easy solution back home: go to the pharmacy down the street from my house, but not in Uganda.

I quickly calculated a ration plan with what I had brought with me; best case, I could last about a month.

"If I ship you some replacement drugs now, would they get there OK considering the time and the heat in transit?" Nita asked. Even that was a gamble.

"I could drastically change my diet, eating nothing that has carbs if I have to for a while. That could buy me another month or so." That plan wasn't realistic either.

Ironically though, this medical dilemma would prove to be the extra force needed to speed the process to our favor. As much as I'd been praying for healing from diabetes these past 15 years, it proved to be an asset that got the U.S. government to move more rapidly.

"I'm going to start calling everyone in the morning and see what we can get going now," she said. "I even know a patient who is a doctor over there. I'll see if there is a way to get an insulin supply to you in a pinch from in country."

She paused. "So how is William?"

"You know, I don't think any of this really affects him, so long as I am here. Just my presence seems to confirm to him that somehow, some way, everything will work out. It's weird how he goes through the catastrophic emotions, once again grabs a death-defying grip on his faith, and then just moves on. I got a lot to learn from this kid."

Later, when I broke the news to Brian and Angela, she offered up the first solution to our crisis.

"We'll come get you and bring you back," she said. "And then we'll figure out what to do next, O.K.?"

Her words weren't those "God will provide" Christianeze crap, they were simply, "Here's a cup of water. Drink." Just what I needed.

I called Nita again, just to hear a voice from home. That insatiable hole of missing home started to dig its way deeper now than at any other time we'd been away from each other, in part because of this deployment's grand uncertainty. This new journey had no end date, no promise of completion, and for that matter, no real immediate goal. During her day, while I was asleep, Nita began spreading the latest news in hopes of doing some slash burning on the potential oncoming firestorm. She had called everyone but the smoke jumpers.

"I am going to call our senator's office on Monday morning," Nita said. "They must be able to do something."

As we spoke further about the challenges ahead and all of the other options that could be in play now, she leveled with me with my decision on that grimy street in the heat of the moment, just outside the Embassy: to stay and make this happen. To bring William home. It was confirmation we were still doing the right thing.

"This was the only decision you could have made," she said. "It was the only one to make. We're just going to have to deal with it, clear to the end. I believe this is what and where God wanted all along."

I agreed.

"I gotta' say though, I'm a little miffed at God though. I still think He could've made this whole thing a little easier."

I was on God's trail all right, I just didn't like this particular bend around rocks where I couldn't see what was ahead.

There were, several "I love you's" and "we'll get through this" sentiments passed back and forth, but as I hung up the phone, the feeling of utter loneliness was overwhelming. Calling someone on the moon would have felt more intimate.

Brian and Angela picked us up the next day. Providentially, the following day was Sunday. They invited us to a church called River of Life where many local Muzungu missionaries attend. It's down the hill a few clicks from Masaka in a rough suburb of Nyendo right on the main road hidden amongst welding shops, boda boda parts houses, furniture grocery shops and a couple of coffin makers.

That Sunday I also met one of the pastors, a local guy named David. I also met Rob and Tim, two guys from the U.K. church who had planted River of Life and their wives and kids. Rob is one of those entrepreneurs of the faith. He's always got something brewing, growing, working behind the scenes for the good within the community. The church had a barracks on the property and was beginning to take in street kids, train and bring them up through a two- year discipleship and schooling program. He was pretty excited about this program and about a number of other works and then said something about prison ministry.

"Hey if you need any help with that, or if I could someday go in, sign me up," I said. "Back home a friend and I have been doing prison ministry on the inside for nearly five years."

"Brilliant!" Rob cheered in the British brogue of his. "Brilliant!... Well, it looks like you're going to be here for at least a few months, so we can see what God does with you then, eh?"

"Whoa, I don't know about a few months, Rob," I said. "I never signed up for a few months of this. Maybe a few miraculous weeks, but not months."

"We shall see."

With nothing happening on Monday, I started a morning Bible study with Brian, William, Edward and his friend Jerrol. The first day, Edward spoke on being real.

"You know David, the spirit man can go beyond the physical man," he said. "This is where your strength is, David, because it is what we really are. We can't fake God because by doing so, it's not being honest to our true self, that's why we fail."

Certainly, "failure" was in my lunch box sealed tight in a Zip-loc baggie. Further, I was also trying to fake a happy smile in the face of what was looking to be the most miserable Christmas of my life. He then read his journal entry for the day. The words hit me like when a preacher makes a side comment and you feel it's meant for you and no one else in a thousand-seat auditorium.

"Work on your deposits. You can't withdraw where you didn't invest. Be the best you were created to be."

Am I in? Or opting out? Am I all in? It's one or the other.

William added his entry into the mix saying that many people are now watching us. Some are ready to make a judgment on what is real, others, whether we will ultimately be successful or fail in our journey of faith.

"If we believe Jesus, He will go ahead of us and do the work necessary for lives to be changed way beyond our own," he said. "If we go forward with disbelief or with our self-appointed way, many lives that would have been touched will not be. Those who are waiting to be 'born again,' then will not."

After the men left through the compound gate and down the dirt drive to the Katweh town traffic circle a few hundred yards away, I felt the need to find a mount of olives. Now.

I headed up the hill. Alone. There was a college at the top with bald patch of grass opening to a view to the south in the direction of Lake Victoria. I needed a word. With God.

And I got it. A clear, soothing voice. A solid direction of inspiration, despite the final destination still unknown. There was now something solid to grab onto, even though I had no idea where it was going to take me.

That's what surrender looked like then. Give up everything I'm trying to man-handle. Quit trying to push the current of the river. Let Him have it. This was my white-flag moment.

In the stillness and the currents of that hilltop air I heard, "Let go of career and family for a season. Let go of those expectations of who you are and what people think. Let me have the dire demand of making money on your behalf. Allow me to have it all. I need you to surrender and be blessed so I can bless those around you as they surrender also."

"So what if I die on this hill, Lord?" I whispered into the breeze.

The next statement wasn't something I heard with my ears. Instead, it was a resonance that happened below where I breath. In the pit of my chest. Beneath my heart, tucked under that inaccessible place deep in, and behind my ribs.

"It would be the noble-est act of courage for my sake. And nothing would make me prouder."

Who knows how many moments passed on top of that hill, but on the slow walk down that afternoon, my phone went off in my pocket. Alarmed at the realization that someone would be calling me in Africa, I caught the name on the caller screen. It was Rob, from River of Life Church, whose number I plugged in yesterday.

"Hey Dave, I've been in a leader's meeting most of the afternoon and all of us couldn't help notice that your name kept coming up."

"I'm not sure what you mean, Rob."

"Our church does this annual conference at the Masaka prison and it's this Thursday. Our speaker has cancelled at the last moment and I can't fill in either. But I was wondering if you would be interested in bringing the word to a couple of hundred men and women inmates at this conference?"

I was shell-shocked and caught completely off guard, not only at the speed of which God was working, but also of the people he was quickly bringing in around me, sending me in a completely foreign direction. From self pity to a platform of speaking, all in a matter of days. All after giving it all up.

When I stood before those prisoners, there wasn't anything else in my hands left to give up to God. Every seed I had been holding onto was gone, either cast aside or burned within the initial fires of this new struggle. One was surely being planted though, in the soil of His choosing, in that microphone. Whatever I was there for was about to be watered, grown, tended and controlled, by Him.

At that moment, the hilltop surrender was real. The condemnation of defeat from feeling like I had lost a battle was no more. God was validating my faith as I was joining Him in His work. His path. A better path. A path I had no idea where it was going or when it would end, but the right path.

I looked over the mob of yellow and realized I was standing and adopted into an extension of my gospel family I had never realized existed. Facing the bright sunshine of golden uniforms worn by spiritually hungry kinsmen imprisoned for sins of the flesh, all waiting to hear something hopeful and eternal, from an unwilling white guy. Me. All of it, incapable of happening, until I submitted to His needs.

When I took my first breath and brought the microphone to my mouth, it hit me that I was here to teach what He had orchestrated in such a bizarre way, against even my own will. I knew for certain, I was in the right place at the right time

I knew I was going to be here, in this place, on this path, for as long as He needed.

It was a white flag moment of surrender. And victory, too.

17

A GOOD SIGN

Since my midnight call to Nita telling her of the bad news, she had been beating the phone warpath since.

The first public official Nita rang up was our district representative, the one we voted for, which I will not name just in case he plans to run for re-election. It was a brief call. "No," she was told. The office didn't have time to look into the matter.

The next office of the people was in the state senate office. They said they would gladly look into the case, but due to the pending holiday break and a thick backlog of business already ahead of us, they couldn't even start on the issue until mid-to-late January. But just before Nita signed off with the senator's secretary, she recommended a friend at the opposing party's office who might be able to help.

Having no help from our own voter alliances, the bipartisan biathlon began. Nita jumped ship, speed-dialed the friend, who turned out to be the lifeline to this whole story. The angel at our registered opposing party's office was a tenacious, thoroughly organized and compassionate woman. Her name was Chris, who worked for Senator Ron Wyden's office in Portland.

Chris promised to work with us any way she could and wanted to get started before everyone left for the holiday break in a few days.

Relieved and hopeful that someone had our same urgent timeline, Nita put a package in the mail that day, wrapping it with a long prayer before dropping in the blue post office box.

She also caught Bev, the home study woman, just before she shut down for the end of the year. What we needed now was the full-meal adoption study, a lot of which she already had. The most urgent item left to get the file complete was fingerprints from both of us so an FBI check could be made.

The only place I could get fingerprints done was back in Kampala, back at the Embassy, which had just closed till the first of the year. By the time I could get fingerprinted and ship the forms back to Nita, it would be mid-January at best.

However, just before I left, both of us had gone down to the local sheriff's office and had fingerprints taken for another matter. Although the clerk who scanned my mitts claimed they don't keep them on file, it was worth a quick check.

Nita raced to the Sheriff's office and arrived only hours before the files were being expunged from the computer system. We were able to get copies of both sets. The only problem was, we both had to sign our individual cards to make them valid.

"Just go into my business cupboard and trace my signature off one of my check carbons and send the package off," I said urgently to Nita at our next phone call. "Babe, every day counts! If we can get just a slight jump on this by the end of the year, get the stuff to the senator's secretary faster, we could cut some serious time off if you just sign my card for me."

"I can't do that," she said. "If anything is suspected as fraud, it would ruin everything and could take even longer for you to get home. I will send it to you express mail."

"Do you have any idea what that will cost?" I pressed.

"I've already checked. $300. But I can also put some of your insulin drugs in the package."

As we scurried to jump through the U.S. government's 10 hoops, more people began following our plight on Facebook. It gave me a brief warm fuzzy knowing that our experiences were still of some interest to others, but I didn't think it would blossom beyond that.

Brian and Angela were planning a last shopping trip back to Kampala the day before Christmas Eve. If there was one thing I had a lot of, unlike my life back in the states, it was time. William and I hopped into the van that morning with their two kids and that adorable rescued Ugandan boy, JoJo. He was so excited at the prospect of seeing Santa Claus that he bounced up and down in the seat for the entire three-hour trek.

It was William's first Christmas too. William had never heard of Santa Claus and didn't really know what to expect. Frankly, neither did I. Back home Santa helpers were white, fat, gut belly laughing, gray haired and bearded types wearing candy cane socks, who were all part of the national Santa's union. Who knows what the Ugandan version would look like?

Upon arriving at the main entrance to the four-story mall, there was no sign of St. Nick. No assigned chair. No elf standing near an instant Polaroid camera. No ringing bells. No signs, except, there was Christmas music playing over the crackly, and distorted speakers.

I had a little money left over from my last bank withdrawal and planned to buy William his first Christmas present. The task proved to be challenging. Especially when William follows so closely on my hip everywhere I went.

After we had snagged some soft-served ice cream, we moseyed into a higher end shoe store. William had never worn a new pair of dress shoes before. The best pair of shoes he'd ever owned were the Nike cross-trainers we had left on the previous trip, and they were already well worn through.

He put his foot hesitantly into the steel foot measurer like it was a some sort of critter trap, and discovered he was a size eight-and-a-half .

"Is that good, dad?" he asked, looking up at me for some sort of approval.

I licked my vanilla cone and chuckled.

He really liked a pair of brown, lace-up, loafer-type shoes. I played real coy that I didn't have enough money and that maybe Santa would have to get those for him. He didn't grasp onto the whole "Santa" mystery, the guy-with-the-sleigh and eight-tiny-reindeer getting him gifts from the North pole sort of thing. But hey, he had ice cream, and he had me, and for the moment life seemed pretty merry.

Angela, bless her heart, had already gotten William a bag full of stocking fun-fillers, candy, dart guns and all the spoiled kid stuff, including an enormous flying foam Frisbee.

If it wasn't for her "mom gears" helping out and keeping me focused on the blessing of the holiday, it would have been a dismal first Christmas for William. She even had some leftover Christmas paper for me to gift wrap William's shoes, which I did so myself, thank you.

Nita was doing the best she could to finish up the holiday errands. It seemed everywhere she stopped, be it the grocery store down the street or a restaurant that knew us well, they all asked, "when are they coming back?"

The practiced, brief and complicated story was told over and over, sometimes with contained emotion and sometimes not, but the sharing would nearly always result in a hug of support and love for her. Phone pictures of well-wishers in those moments started to collect and get forwarded. There were some with Santa hats, hand-made signs reading "missing you," and staged goofiness that were intended to send a hug our way, too.

Our usual home routine for the Christmas Eve was this: Nita's parents and extended family come over to one of the houses for food and the traditional white-elephant gift game hilarity. My son, Garrett had been dating a young woman, Bethany, who he was bringing home for the festivities, a first for him. Also, my daughter, Mikayla and her fiancé Zack would be there. It would have been a first for us having both of our kids with their "potential significant others" on display for the whole extended family. And William and I would be missing that.

Nita hosted 20 guests on Christmas Eve but not neat as it was to have the kids' significant others on hand, she "just wasn't feeling it."

I wasn't feeling the jingle in my bells this particular Christmas morning, either. We SKYPED with Nita and the kids and others while they did the Eve thing with the time difference. At one point, they set the laptop down on the counter and William and I watched people graze in and out of the food area around the dining room. Then randomly someone would poke their heads into the screen and shout something rhetorical. It was like a bad reality TV show, entertaining somewhat, but way more awkward than usual.

One of the most meaningful moments for me that Christmas was a simple ornament made by Bethany. She hung it on the home tree and sent me a picture of it on Facebook: It featured a brown paper cut-out of the African continent that was slipped inside like a ship in a bottle. A tiny red heart was placed right about where the country of Uganda sits and surrounding it were the carefully penned words, “I will not leave you as orphans, I will come to you,” taken from the scripture in John 14:18.

The image hit me right where I was hurting the most. It not only took my breath and stole a tear, but whittled away at some of my resentment as well. The scripture was one I had shared with her during a time of trial when Bethany had come to Three Sixteen church months ago, after the death of her first husband, at age twenty-four. Those words were offered to her during a very dark time in her faith as well. Now she was passing them back as a sign of encouragement and faithfulness during my own sunless winter.

William’s stocking and the contents from Angela were a huge hit. The western tradition of each person within the family having a stocking was a sign that he belonged somewhere, finally. Even if where he was really going, hadn’t happened yet.

The last gift he opened was the shoes. As he carefully tore the paper, even though the tag said it was from Santa, he said right away, “You’re Santa, right, Dad?”

And like I’ve lied for years, I took the fifth, silence, just shrugged my shoulders through the excited ripping as he got down to the bare shoe box. Wait for it. There it is, that buggy-eyed wonder of realizing what he had in his hands was totally unexpected.

“It’s those shoes I tried on the other day isn’t it?” totally surprised and wide-eyed. “How did you get those without me knowing about them?”

“It’s Christmas magic,” I said. “That’s the small part Santa’s do for the ones they love, William. In fact, they’ll do most anything, just like Jesus, who is the reason for today.”

Sometime during the opening of gifts that evening when we were Skyping U.S. time Christmas morning, William had slipped off. Unbeknownst to me he had gathered some of his colored pencils and paper that Angela had put in his stocking, and made a sign of his own.

It proved to be his way of speaking through all of the past disappointments and the coming wrestling's, that the signs of success were everywhere. There were signs of care surrounding us, and the sign of victory was soon to come. So he made his sign.

When I came back to the bedroom, stuck to the door with scotch tape were the colorful letters centered beautifully on the plain white paper, lit by a one fluorescent bulb.

"Dad and William's room."

I read it aloud a few times, followed by a hug from him. It was a hug from a skinny young orphaned boy, who was no longer, orphaned.

"Merry Christmas, Dad," he said looking up at me.

"Merry Christmas, son," I said.

18

WEEDS AND EGGS

Weeding beet fields was my summer job during middle school. Easy work. Straddle the rows to pull the weeds early spraying didn't catch.

One field didn't get sprayed and was overgrown and infested. The work, much harder, the weeds taller and the pace slower without an ending date in sight. But weeding the entire field was necessary for the crop to survive. Daily appreciation was tough to muster, until the last morning we were there.

The old farmer said weeds gone from a field make the landscape very beautiful. "It's a God kind of beauty," he said. His perspective and the daily change to the landscape by my labor and time made me appreciate being in that different field. I learned to value the struggle. And what the struggle produced.

Likewise, I found myself laboring in a very different field after that Christmas in Uganda. There were days that I agonized to see the value in any of it, until I started developing eyes with the ability to see the beauty after plucking through the weeds.

We started a weekly routine to Skype into the church on Sunday mornings for a continued presence from the bi-vocational pastor. Quite often, during phone calls to Nita prior to such messages, she would hear the details of my new lows and respond with her overly-compassionate words, "you better just get it together before Skyping in for Sunday service."

Those words from her were blunt, and harsh, but I was in those kind of rows and God knows I needed them. My weedy rows were in a much larger field than I'd ever been before. But is was becoming apparent that it was all part of His process. Keep walking forward in this new field, pull the weeds, repeat until the field was clean.

The visa/immigration work being done for William's adoption was mostly generated from stateside efforts. Nita's efforts. The exception being if there were a few documents needing my original signature. Over the Christmas weeks, Nita and I both teamed up, divided and conquered the first item on the checklist of to-dos. We logged online and within a few days, had gone through the required education modules for "new" parents. We got a number of chuckles from the whole "new parent" thing.

There was a series of seven modules. All question and answer formats, which covered everything from medical emergencies, overcoming identity issues, cultural changes when moving to a new home, when to take an adoptee to Costco (not to blow their minds too early), and finally, what to do if the new family member started setting small fires in their bedroom.

There wasn't a module for the man stuff. So I took it upon myself to teach William the most important man rule. Put the toilet seat down. I was surprised at the difficulty to learning this.

"This is the number one rule of the household," I said. "If you forget everything else I'm going to teach you, this is the rule that will always save your bacon."

"What's bacon?" he asked.

"Ah, my good son, they are smoked pork strips from heaven," I said. "Trust me, we will definitely learn that glorious benefit of food sparkle later and often. But don't ever forget law number one. The lid always goes down when you're done. Everything else can be forgiven, this task deserves your utmost focus and diligence."

Pastor Edward invited me to preach at some rural churches and to bring William along, too. While driving out to one of his churches, Pastor Edward told me that recently he'd been praying for my ministry, as he says God is revealing to him. He said it was changing the men in Uganda.

"You are now a father to William and now you have bonded yourself to be a father to Uganda." Nothing like a little prophecy to put you into an unfamiliar field, where you see nothing but weeds, while someone else sees nothing but beautiful produce and fruit.

With me immersed in local ministries, that first week of waiting went by so fast that we almost missed the call from the DHL shipping clerk the next Friday. Our fingerprint forms that needed signing had arrived. A polite woman on the phone said that the small box only needed another $80 for it to clear the customs tag that was slapped on it. Nearly $400 for my signature.

I was expecting an envelope, but instead it was a small box jammed with all kinds of thoughtful candies from home, some playing cards, a Yatzee electronic game, some photos and some freeze-dried survival foods like, chili, and a large packet of southwestern spiced eggs.

Hence, the customs charge. I signed the documents and quickly made a rendezvous with a cab courier back to Entebbe Airport that evening. Hopefully, Nita would have those cards in her hand soon to start the first governmental grind to the process of William's immigration.

We took our newly arrived booty to the apartment from that first DHL shipment and laid it all out on the coffee table like pirates treasure. Agreeing to "ration" the sweets and the beef jerky, which were all new tastes to William. We were excited to try the Spanish spiced eggs for breakfast the next morning. If we couldn't have pancake Saturday, then freeze-dried eggs were going to be the highlight to the weekend.

According to the directions, the eggs had to soak in water for a half-hour so that the beans in the mix could fully swell before heating. I meticulously measured out the water, placed the pan on the cold hot plate to warm later, and went outside on the porch to journal in my Bible.

About 15 minutes later, I heard William digging around in the kitchen and then in bathroom as part of his morning routine. I was nearly finished journaling when I started to smell burning eggs. I raced into the kitchen to see the pot of eggs. Those golden, beautifully photographed and packaged, U.S. made, Mexican spiced Huevos Rancheros were smoldering away on a hot plate burner with the dial set to incinerate. My desire for that little taste of home I'd been craving for over a month was about to be fed to the dogs.

"What happened?"

"Oh, I thought you forgot to turn on the burner," William said, "so I turned it on for you."

"But you were just in the shower, right?"

"Yes I was. I must have forgot that I turned the burner on."

My emotional containment mechanisms were failing at space shuttle reentry speeds. Maybe from all of the little letdowns, and uncertainties and delays they all came out in one big ball of fiery furor.

"Why? Why?" I stumbled for the last bit of lid pressure to keep what I wanted to say under wraps, but I blew it royally.

"You've ruined our breakfast. You burnt our eggs and what's more you just did it and don't *remember*!"

I can't imagine what William was feeling, but by the drop in his face muscles, I could tell he was falling into the nearest black hole of rejection. He left the room to finish getting dressed and then went out to the front porch. I hurriedly attempted to soft land and salvage the debris of the breakfast crash with whatever good pieces were left.

Handing William his plate as he sat on the step, I eased into the wicker porch chair careful not to spill my hot tea. The morning sun was filtering through the tree. It's yellow rays were dappling his tear-stained face. We were eating this breakfast that was supposed to be the highlight of our weekend and I found myself in a place I couldn't seem to break free from.

I started to weep as my heart began to break from self justification that was morphing into shame. I could see and sense the pain of William's wounded feelings like it was my own father coming down hard on me for something that was an innocent lapse of good intention.

Coming down off my elevated chair, I sat right next to him and put my arm around his narrow little shoulders, across a new shirt we had just gotten the day before at the market.

"I'm so sorry," I said. "The stress of all this and the wait is tearing me up. But I want you to know, you are, and will always be, more important than burnt eggs.

"My emotions are so hurt for this failure and for you, and I'm trying to be strong during the things we are having to endure, William, that I took all of that out on you. And that's not right."

Before I could even ask, he said, "I forgive you, Dad. God will get us through this."

For me, this became a major turning point. All of my fight wasn't going to change the field I was in. Nothing was going to make it magically weed-free without the required labor of dealing with the infestations that were right in front of me. I could however, destroy the row I was on and the beauty of the whole field by not yanking that one chest-high weed that would ruin the landscape.

I was in the right mission field all right, and at the same time, the mission field was in me. The pay was rough, but the steady value was being made everyday I showed up to work.

There was grand beauty yet to be seen, just like the farmer who looked at the finished field after our days of labor. But there were many a weeds left to pulled.

Especially the ones still on my row.

19

NITA AND THE GARBAGE

While William and I were adapting to bachelor life, finding more ways to get involved in where God was working, we were really in a holding pattern. The real and necessary work was being done stateside by Nita.

So for the next two-plus months she was bearing the load of getting us home. At the expense of writing a book on "the preaching life of David and William" I wanted to give her an opportunity to express her point of view. The sizzle of the story centers on the drama of William and me stuck in Africa. But let's not forget the real and important paper battle was being waged by Nita, who kept going to work as a dental hygienist, kept cutting through the adoption bureaucratic barriers, kept propping me up when I was weak and weary. Not to mention the woman who rallied a faithful posse to pray for our safe and successful return home.

To be fair, her work was the most crucial work. Her struggles over the long haul were just as real and just as painful. So, I wanted you to hear from her for the next two chapters.

What gets cloudy about this whole story is when people are more sympathetic and "wow-ed" by the part where William and David were stuck in Africa for three months. While they were adapting to a life over there, an equal amount of fight was happening here in the form of red tape. I was rallying to get help, keep the governmental gears grinding, and struggling to buck up and surrender to this new field in which I found myself.

Like most busy people and working couples, David and I juggle a number of different ventures between us. We have established our individual routines based on the strengths of what each one does well. So this means a number of jobs hang in the balance with the prolonged absence of the other. They can easily become burdensome additions that were never on the other person's radar, or in his or her gift set. Each and everyone of his tasks, I now found myself having to master, in addition to my own set of regular household duties.

But since we've left that life, our gender roles and gift sets had been re-adapted and more equally redistributed. I've only mowed the lawn maybe four times in all of our marriage, and I don't lift up the hood on my car anymore when it sputters. Case in point, when I'm gone, David never gets the mail. Bills, checks and department store coupons never seem to get out of the post box, which is located right at the end of our 25-foot driveway.

Rolling the garbage to curbside by 6 a.m. every Tuesday has long been David's job. While backing out of the driveway on my way to work before dawn that morning, my headlights flashed across the street over to the garbage and recycling containers at the end of neighbor's driveway. I, for the first time, noticed there were a number of those lining our street. Sighing deeply, I clutched the steering wheel, realizing everything about the house and life without my spouse was now entirely my responsibility. I had to deal with all of the daily and weekly garbage, including the stuff in the those green and blue rolling totes.

Luckily that morning, Kevin, our neighbor across the driveway, was also work-bound on his way to drive the city's buses.

"Hey, neighbor," I called out through the dark and the fog, "If you notice that I'm not participating in any of the normal neighborhood activities, such as getting the weekly garbage to the curb, could you just feel free to come over and get it for me, as you would be right in assuming I've totally gaffed it?"

He didn't catch my humor right at first, but instead, took it seriously to task. From that morning on, Kevin took on the watch of getting my garbage to the curb faithfully every Tuesday morning. Thorough, and loyal to a "T," he was one of a growing handful of people that God was lining up to become an integral part of the William story, and heart. He was the initial signal that I wasn't left alone, or orphaned. Later and overwhelmingly, I found there was a safety net of many people waiting to step in to help, bless us and be blessed as well. God was starting to bring together lots of hands willing to join in the battle for our family.

Chris, the lady we joined forces with from Senator Ron Wyden's office, became a critical cog in the story in a huge way. She became my new e-mail and phone BFF. With all of the goings on with the Homeland Security, Immigration and FBI background checks, plus the multiple layers of bureaucracy we were wading through, she was the one who stayed on top of it all. Chris would e-mail me multiple times a week giving me progress reports on all of the immigration documents she was pushing hard through the slow gears of government. Additionally, she was there if something I had missed needed re-scanning or re-filing because things routinely got "misplaced" in the system or jammed up somewhere along the way. She was also a great source of compassion and emotional encouragement during those phone calls of "good news, bad news."

She continued to push the lethargic governmental system through the red-tape maze in such an elegant way that nobody seemed to get angry with her steam-engine kind of persistence. If I had been on the other end of some of those phone calls and e-mails, with my mama bear claws out, plus my frequent hot-flashes, there would have been heads of office people rolled up and collected in a pile somewhere in a secluded place off the grid for sure.

Bev, who initially did the scaled-down home study, came back again to aid right away, too. She completed a full adoption packet in near record time and then continued to help steer the state requirements through the slalom courses on our behalf too. This feisty lady really helped when something unusual was required at the last minute by some state paper jockey who thought all these people rallying and converging for a single case just might be doing something fishy.

Which is why Bev called one Thursday afternoon now needing more letters of reference. ASAP. They had to be filed before some phantom Friday deadline to get us another needed state certification. I got our clutch friends, Bob and Mary in California to write one, along with my understanding employer John, and a pastor friend of ours in Los Angeles who was in the middle of college finals. *Oh, by the way, I pleaded, can you have that on my e-mail server before you all go to bed tonight?*

Granted, these are all busy people with harried lives like the rest of us, going in all kinds of directions. When I asked them for a letter, rushed and the content of "it-better-be-good," they were more than willing to forgive my "drop-everything-it's-about-me" request and all of them came through. They even helped route the correspondences to all the places they needed to go. I just wished the electronic system within the government was that accommodating and efficient.

My friend Mary, right after sending her reference letter, hopped on the next plane out of LA. She ended up spending a week with me right when I was needing someone to lean on the most. As I write this, I want her to know that our 30-plus-year friendship has been one of the greatest gifts of my life. That week you dropped everything and came to Oregon, got me through one of the most emotionally demanding stretches of stress and fragile emotions of my life. My sincerest "Thank You" is a mere shadow of my immense gratitude for that gesture.

After the letters were off, Mary and I drove an hour north a few days later, to get the finished and now state-approved copy of our full home study from Bev. She had already uploaded the packet to the U.S. Homeland Security people and now we needed to ship David a certified copy for the Ugandan Embassy file. When Bev handed the file to us, she held on, as I tried a second time, to pull it from her hands.

"I want to pray over this one too, please," she insisted.

With that, the three of us moms, petitioned to the highest court in the kingdom for help, wisdom, victory and any speed the Almighty could offer. It was one of those moments I will never forget, and I'm certain it was powerful and effective in the process.

It never ceased to amaze me, that just when we're trying to beat some sort of deadline, some unexplained freak of nature would swirl it. I recall sending one document four separate times, then following-up with a number of phone calls, just to make sure it was received and put on the right person's desk at the top of the stack in the right file. And then another Tuesday would come around, and more garbage in those rolling totes would have to go to the curb.

I didn't have a clue how to keep David's commercial photography business and rental properties businesses going, but, as with the whole bring-William-to-America challenge, you just find a way.

A bank teller we've known for years, Sumin, once asked me how everything was going. I started to say the usual "fine" courtesy response, but things weren't fine and frankly, I was tired of lying about it to everyone for the past two months. She already knew in an instant things weren't "fine" because, looking at the items on her counter, she knew things were already being done wrong.

"When David normally makes these deposits he has a sheet of paper of what he wants done with them," Sumin said. "Is he not back yet?"

"It's been tough lately," I managed to admit. "David's still in Uganda and I'm struggling to figure out how he does things. He's still in Uganda and has hit some immigration snags. We really have no idea when he and William are going to be home."

She gasped. Being from Indonesia and being far away from her own extended family, she instantly understood the scope of my troubles, even if she didn't realize this was only the tip of my iceberg.

David's car had just died in the driveway a few days before when someone borrowed it; no fault of theirs. Also, one of the renters had given notice to vacate in the next two weeks. The small commercial space with a hair salon didn't have heat on one of the coldest weeks of the winter and the other café tenant had just called to tell me her HVAC system had been making funny noises for the past four days. Suddenly, my car was sputtering and the check engine light came on just as I was idling up to the bank window. When it rains, it pours.

Sumin looked at me and the stack of confusion in front her. "Here, let me take care of this," she said. A few moments later, she slid back the checkbooks and motioned toward a hand-written sticky note and drawn smiley face on top of the stack.

"I gave you my personal cell phone number and contact information at the bank, plus my work schedule for the next few weeks. Call me if you need anything. I know how David takes care of these accounts and I can do all of this for you. Please, allow me to help."

"Thank you, I will," I said. Because she was such a great source of information, I was almost tempted to ask her if she knew where David took our car to get fixed.

Sumin turned out to be one of many great helps of the crisis. Thanks to her, we bounced no checks, missed no payments, nor did I screw anything up beyond fiscal repair.

As I pulled out of the drive-way that day I felt at odds with what to tackle next. There were still so many balls in the air and upcoming concerns on my plate. My daughter's summer wedding, her last semester of college tuition due soon, house maintenance expenses, and those continual and mounting adoption costs.

At least the garbage was being taken care of.

20

CRISES SQUARED

It's been said that crisis comes in threes or fours. The garbage was only the first.

We'd already gotten David his insulin and diabetic supplies covering the first crisis, but the longer and looming worry was how to stretch the finances.

Mikayla, our daughter, was living 45 minutes to the north at college, finishing up her last terms as a nuclear radiation health physics major. (Yes, it is as expensive as it sounds.) She couldn't seem to bring herself to tell me she needed the next semester's tuition right after the New Year holiday.

Thankfully, we had the funds already put aside, barely—but the day she called she was all giggles and grins because out of the blue, we had our first ever tuition grant dropped into her college account! To celebrate, she even came down to have dinner with me and helped mail David's next package: Valentine underwear, hearts and candies with cards we had people sign.

Mikayla is also an advanced organizer. It was January. Her August wedding seemed to be nearing faster than we might get the boys home. Between booking venues, arranging flowers, bridesmaid dresses, and all of that, it was good to have such a great planner in the family instead of a needy "bridezilla." Of the two kids, she seemed to be the most excited about getting another brother, re-sharing everything David posted to Facebook and pulling in prayers from all the people on her friends list.

Still in the midst of that winter cold-snap, bad timing issues came steadily. I had noticed the water in our outside green house slowly came to a crawl with its water pressure and then a day or two later, just quit working all together. The heater was working overtime trying to keep the plants from dying. It was still 20 degrees outside, and I was really beginning to wish I was somewhere else.

Despite moving soon to Central Oregon to be closer to Bethany and snow-boarding slopes, Garrett stepped up to do the "honey-do" stuff.

He had just run a successful Kickstarter internet capitol funding campaign to launch his bag company, July Nine. With nearly 50K in orders the first month, he was trying to turn a manufacturing hail storm out of the other half of our garage. If he had any spare time he was spending it with a fabulous young girl he had met on a photo shoot with dad a year or so earlier. It's a wonder the kid could think straight, but I'm glad he did.

Garrett knew how David ran the rentals when a tenant gave notice. He's a business minded young man and is really tight with his dad. He quickly put up an ad on CraigsList and within a couple of days had the place signed and buttoned up with a minimum of turnover hassle. I didn't even have to go clean out the stove or refrigerator, which I despise and refuse to do. It was my suggestion to put on the leases to charge double the cleaning fee against the security deposit, just in case you're thinking of renting from me. Not sure if that's what David does. But oh, well.

With the bone-chilling weather, it was only a matter of time before another rental problem erupted, like a heating unit at the cafe. I sifted through David's Iphone and called his contractor, who was sick with the flu. There was nothing I could do but that didn't seem to stop the persistent messages from the tenant. I suggested they try a few plug-in space heaters for a while.

The following day however the heating contractor rallied himself out of bed and got over to take a look at the problem. Instead of a little gratitude, the tenant leveled her heating frustrations onto him. Not feeling up to the abuse, he understandably threw his hands up and loaded up his tools, refusing to work with that, quote, "b**ch" without an apology. As he was telling me this sordid tale I was having another hot flash, and at the same time, I found myself hoping the tenant was having a hot flash too. Then maybe the brewing heat problem would be solved.

My cell phone jingled and I found myself playing United Nations envoy in a playing field that's not usually mine. Renters and contractors. I decided to pay her a visit.

The café owner vocally reiterated to me that it had indeed been four days that her customers were dealing with the HVAC issue and it had gone on too long.

I took a deep breath for the sake of control, digested the contents of her comments, before I outlined my fragile emotions back at her.

"You know I've been waiting 74 days for my issue to be fixed and I see no end in sight," I said, with all the pieces of calm restraint I could muster.

"I call your three-days or even four. And raise you 74. Fair enough?" I said with my index finger pointing into her personal bubble, when it appeared that possibly her curtness wasn't going to be curtailed.

In short, an apology was given to the HVAC guy and within the hour, the heat was restored, the rest of the excess roasting cooled off quickly as well.

The yellow light on my car was flickering, which according to David is the signal of death. Steady light, OK. A flickering check engine light however, is the sign to pull over and call the tow truck, so that's what I did. Now when my car goes to the shop, it's never an eighty-dollar fix, that's half an oil change. Sure, at that time, my car was 11 years old, and needing some maintenance attention, but it was deemed reliable and a safe tank for me and the kids, (by David of course, because cars are his department).

The bill came back and I had to revisit the bank and go a little deeper into the savings account. Thank God he had stashed some extra money away before leaving to Africa. I didn't tell him the real invoice cost, nothing he could do about it anyway.

Our friend Bob, who is a Harley Davidson guru and our church finance guy, came over to put David's motorcycle battery on charge. He was worried that his bike was getting mistreated, neglected, lonely, or cold. Bob hooked up some cables, plugged them in and then lovingly covered the motorcycle in a warm fuzzy blanket. He then made the mistake of asking me how I'm doing and listened to me lament over the car and rental issues.

Weeks of this sort of routine continued. Crisis, wait, somebody shows up to take care of it. Another crisis, more wait, another person in the story. More wait. People stepped in at the right time, crisis gone. Breathe and wait some more.

I would mindlessly go to work to pick teeth and suck spit, my Dental Hygienist duties, then work on the home stuff the minute I got off, handling mine and David's usual duties. My phone was always near my dental cubicle, just in case a critical call came in. John, my doctor-boss, waited many times to do exams because I often put him late on his schedule answering crisis calls. All of my patients were sympathetic to the breaks in professionalism when I had to sporadically de-glove myself and halt their cleanings to answer the phone. People became wrapped up in the story by the minute-by-minute events. There were many crucial mountains climbed, and several low valleys, many of us walked together.

When things tended to go a little quiet for a few days, I'd recheck with Chris at the Senator's office. She gave me honest status information and even in the face of bad news, was still an encourager. I remember often Chris would apologetically ask for another piece of paper to be re-scanned. She would say, "check your e-mail I just sent you," with a kindly worded sense of urgency. I would print it out, dash over to my parent's house around the corner from ours after work, scan and e-mail the docs on their computer to get it there just a few minutes before she would leave for the day. Always, she would stay late, and finish my stuff before going home for the evening.

I often thought of her being stuck in more Portland traffic, just because she cared enough to help us, and was sold out to the story, helping William with his brighter future ahead. It's already taking a village to get this kid here, much less raise him.

My parents were getting the latest developments between the cracks in the chaos. They were watching me suffer along, perhaps unnecessarily in their eyes, and seeing me grow more weary along the way. I can't imagine how hard it might have been for them, not understanding at first why we were even doing this adoption in the first place. Why a black kid from Africa was going into a white family of which, generations ahead of mine, had slaves? Talk about your irony. Add to that, their misunderstanding of risking so much of our time, resources, money and lives for a child we barely knew, but knew should be ours.

Even our three regular restaurants we eat out at, got into the story after not seeing David with me for so long. The Mexican place we affectionately call "soggy taco" gave me an occasional on-the-house Margarita when I looked too down. The pizzeria place spotted me a glass of wine or two, (I may have lost the exact count). And the burrito place where our daughter Mikayla used to work, I got a handful of free lunches to help cheer me up on some of those really gray days. The manager, a mom herself with four kids, would even sit with me for a while to catch up on the latest story developments, lending an empathic ear.

Our small church body was also a source of great support. I'm sure they didn't even know how much. Dwayne stepped in and preached the whole time David was gone. He said he was honored to just be able to serve. What a heart!

The worship pastor took over the executive leadership role in stride, and steered the ship steady. Many others stepped up and collectively, the entire body of Three Sixteen Ministries kept persevering even without my input or David's leadership. As much as it seemed the world was revolving around us, it was instead revolving around a God-sized story of faith and promise. It became beat to the hearts of all who hung on the fringes. Every facet of the story touched someone, somehow, in whatever field they found themselves in.

There are a number of other things David just didn't need to know about while he was out of reach and couldn't do anything about. Come to find out, we had a broken water pipe from that year's winter freeze. That's the reason we later found why greenhouse water stopped. It's probably the first he's heard about it, as he reads this draft now. But don't worry honey, you couldn't have fixed from where you were anyway. You didn't need to stress about a frozen pipe, or non-working water, or that new alternator in your car, or the water pump in mine. And you don't need to check any of them now. They're all fixed. Handled. Behind us. At least for now.

There was a lot besides the garbage to be dealt while you and William were in Africa. But in reality, it was the appointed details of God's heart bringing many together for the cause of rescuing this one orphan, our starfish. It was also a test for me to see if I had the legs to walk the entire journey, even if I couldn't see the end of the rainbow either.

Rest assured though, the real garbage always got wheeled to the curb on time, by Kevin, because apparently, Tuesday comes every week.

Which reminds us all that dealing with garbage is a necessity that's always somebody's job, if not everybody's privilege.

At some point, we all find ourselves important contributors in some of the largest stories of life, helping each other with details, saving the day, taking care of the garbage.

And of course, all the other crises that come with it.

21

NO SHORTCUTS

The holidays fell into the rear view mirror and time marched on. That's African time, mind you.

William and I fell into a zone. Life became African. The pace and routine were developed to distract the long waiting and work Nita was doing in the states.

We taught and preached as a trio road show. We rode the shirts tails of Pastor Edward and William served as my trusty English-to-Ugandan interpreter.

Our story was casual conversation on many lips around town and we became known by many shopkeepers and neighborhood residents. Some of our new missionary church contacts were talking to their contacts, who were talking to others, each one asking if anyone knew a way to help us through the sealed hatches of the visa office's labyrinth. From that, I'm sure, raised the temptation of a shortcut that I bit onto when a snake slithered its voice into my mobile phone around late January.

Looking for a shortcut always seems to bring out the predators, wolves, and snakes to the naïve and desperate.

In the depths of the forest of sleaze surfaced a big-time TV evangelist from Kampala. According to him, he had enough influence through his associates to get our visa done and stamped. He told me over the phone that he was confident that if William and I could come to the capitol city and meet him the next day, that he would have us on a plane by week's end.

That kind of temptation is tough to dismiss. I wasn't doing anything that next day, and unexpected news like that could only be a miracle, right?

The morning brought rain the size of water balloons. We exited the bus at the central Kampala taxi park jumping puddles and ducking under make-shift tarp coverings. By the time we navigated the 14 blocks to the hotel where we were meeting this big-shot pastor, we weren't looking our Sunday best.

An assistant of his met us at the lobby entrance and led us into the elevator onto the third floor. In Africa, the term "pastor" has the status of an elected official or a rock star. I've seen women kneel and kiss a pastor's hands, men grovel and run to get coffee. A good many of these guys are nothing more than artisan con men, but, unfortunately, it's hard to tell them apart.

The elevator opened to a waiting area with two sofas and a mismatched chair. I was expecting to go further into an office, or a conference room to meet in, but the assistant quickly glanced around the waiting area and said, "this will be fine, I will call him now."

We milled around while our clothes dried and thirty minutes or so later a man looking a lot like a Las Vegas lounge singer emerged from the doors of the elevator. By the look on his face, I'm sure we weren't what he was expecting either.

After the pastor told me all about his influence, radio and television shows and all of his churches he had planted around the area he finally got around to inquire about my situation. Briefly, I delivered the rehearsed and oft-told saga of William and our God-given calling toward him and all of our roadblocks to getting home. Somewhere in my fantasy thinking, I still believed that this man was here to help us.

"Well, I think I can help you get what you need for this young man, William," he said. "These kind of situations require the help of a few people and—."

Wait for it. I could sense the buzzer.

"I would need some little money to help the process along, you know, to give to the people who will help."

Bam! There it is, the shortcut con!

"Pastor, thank you for your time." I said, abruptly standing and extending my hand toward his gold-ringed fingers resting on his tailored slacks.

"I, too, am a pastor at a church back in my home country. As a pastor, I carry the responsibility of helping people just like you do. Yet, I don't charge for my help, if the help was offered to a person in real need. I figure, if I offer to help, the expenses to do what I have spoken will either be covered by me, or by the Almighty himself. That's called the fellowship of the faith."

I was not catching if he was either puzzled or offended—and didn't care. I had to get this off my chest.

Gathering up my backpack and motioning to William, I continued to rant, pausing just for a moment for the closing last word.

"I am tired of people saying they want to help us and then ask for money before they even start. Why offer? If you offer help to someone where I'm from, then you keep your word and help. It shouldn't ever be about money, but the integrity of your word."

And as if on cue, the elevator door slid opened to let a guest off to their room, thus allowing us a perfectly timed exit. The doors closed and we rode to the lobby.

"Ok, that's it." I said once we got out of the elevator. "No more looking for shortcuts. This is all going to be in God's timing and I'm just going to have to trust that. Again. I'm done wasting time on trying to push the river."

As we reached the street curb, William looked up at me and smirked.

"That man wasn't a good pastor, was he Dad?" he said.

"I don't know if he's good or not." I said. "He's the kind of man who looks for ways to stand up for what he believes without having to really fight for it."

"What do you mean?" he asked.

I told William that God promised in his word, that He would stand up for those who don't have anyone to stand up and fight for themselves. He uses men of God in this fight too, you, Mom, me and everyone else who is willing to stand up and fight for something worthwhile. And He uses those who are willing to do this at great cost to themselves. That's called sacrifice.

"People sacrifice themselves and we want to call them heroes. God calls them the faithful.

"Even if we keep getting knocked down, or go broke, we'll keep getting up believing and standing on the basic promise that God's people always win."

That day was the final reminder that there're no shortcuts to doing the right thing, for the right reason at the right time. There are no painless fights, either. Only honorable sacrifices.

Shortcuts are always a temptation. I mean who wants a battle to last longer than it has to? Which is exactly the point. The important battles need to go the distance. I've found over and over again the length of a battle is predetermined by God himself. I can either face it fully now, or waste time with a short cut that only makes the battle period longer. Shortcuts, shortcut the lesson. It can even extend the misery, and spoil the ultimate victory.

I needed to stay in the zone, this was a predetermined process teaching me honor in sacrifice.

I wasn't just on African time, but God's. There was no shortcutting that.

22

COLLATERAL DAMAGE OF THE FAITH

If ever we thought we were casualties, the mission of bringing William home showed my family and those connected to the story that there are even greater casualties around this story.

As word got out into the community that a gray-haired, apparently well-to-do, Muzungu was fighting to take one of their own out of the country, we began to experience subversive conflict.

This was the piece of the William story that forever connected my family to the country of Uganda. It blew my Christian comfort zone to bits.

Very few of us ever experience real religious persecution. Persecution is more than receiving flack on Facebook. It's facing death for what you profess. Most of us are not even acquainted with the terms "ultimate sacrifice", or even "collateral damage".

Collateral damage. It's a phrase used to describe ill-intentioned harm in a war, being at the wrong place, at the wrong time.

Thus unfolded a significant chapter of the African experience at a church that assembled in the garage of a rented house, where we preached a number of times during our stay. It was the place of Derek, Peace and their mother, Annet.

Back in the corner of a digital photo I snapped that first day we were there preaching were three faces. All three previously unknown. Now, by the light of a single florescent bulb shining through the front door to our porch apartment, I studied those faces with excruciating detail. There were a flood of questions about them, and an arid drought of answers.

Their pixilated images I couldn't help but stare at now, wondering if I could have interceded before the events of the last 48 hours. Or if I had missed something while being oblivious to my own self.

Prior to this event, William and I were feeling increasingly like war had come to our doorstep. As the grind of the adoption process moved through the end of the second month, some of our daily life confrontations, at times, got fierce.

There were blatant cutting in line moves while shopping. Scornful looks, even some so bold as to move my items that were already on the check-out counter, ready to be paid for aside, so they could set theirs in front. The first few times is happened, I let it slide. The last thing I wanted to do was end up in jail standing up for "my rights." But the time was brewing to take some sort of action.

There were direct confrontations in public by testosterone-charged young men, challenging us about the length of William's hair. He had grown it out about an inch in my preparation for an Oregon winter. The head-shaven men felt it necessary to approach us, unprovoked, demanding to me with their pointed fingers in my face that he get him "taken care of." In other words, shave his head like everyone else. Or else.

I wasn't beginning to feel unsafe but oddly, the confrontations seemed to becoming more frequent after the situation with Derek, Peace and their mother, Annet. But, on the other hand, I also never, and I mean never, left the apartment without my trusty Kershaw folding knife secretly clipped inside my hip.

The most personal attack was when Boda drivers from "another faith' played "chicken" one day when we were walking along the road back to the apartment.

William, JoJo and I were walking tight to the left side of the road. College students and motorcycle taxis were busily navigating the center section. JoJo was holding my hand, positioned to the inside with William shielding behind him.

The boda-drivers were coming down the hill and would have kept to the far side of the road, (left hand European rules). Just then, the driver, suddenly and intentionally steered directly for my shoulder. This wasn't my first experience like this. It normally came from the ones who wore multi-colored Kufi hats, but like a good tourist, in the past, I had moved clear off the road.

However, given the circumstances of the previous two days with Derek, Peace and their mother, I was on the jagged edge. My next were going to be my statement for the persecution I'd been a recent witness to against the faith.

"Hey William and JoJo," I yelled over the road noise, establishing a beginning to a totally made-up story. I threw my right arm theatrically away from my side making an exaggerated gesture toward the sky.

As I swung my right arm wide over the roadway, the boda driver couldn't avoid the impending contact. He was about to get "clothes-lined" right off his motorcycle. He tried to veer, ducking his unprotected head and loosing his Kufi. My stiff arm instead, struck his passenger just below the chin, knocking him off the back of the seat.

The driver braked abruptly and started to get off the bike. The passenger had already been dispatched away from the bike, was spun around but still on his feet. *Game on.*

"Hey! What the Hell was that about?" I yelled,

stepping abruptly right to verbal striking range, and around their motorized mosque.

"Who do you think you are?" the passenger shouted back, but before he could catch another breath, I stepped even closer right into fire breathing, uh, prayer range.

"I'm the guy you just tried to hit." I hollered, wanting to include all of the people into voice shot, intending the word got out through the rumor mill.

"I was the guy walking with a three year-old little boy that you nearly took out without thinking."

The driver shuffled in reverse and got back on the motorcycle. It was already creeping down the hill with his passenger friend now revving the throttle. He picked up his Kufi and his friend dropped the clutch the second his butt hit the seat.

"And tell the others I live here!" I shouted down the hill as they disappeared into the dust and pedestrians.

"Hey dad, that guy was Muslim, wasn't he," William said. I didn't answer. I didn't need to.

The first time we preached at the garage church, Annet went home that day celebrating. Her excitement was for all the blessings that had come her way, getting Pastor Edward to come to the village for a bible study, and now a visiting pastor from America was there too. The church had also grown into a full-fledged congregation with a pastor and a few men overseers. A real church. All because of her.

In Africa, this is big news. It was like a spiritual badge of honor. She shared the jubilation that day with her husband, who, by the way, was same faith as the boda drivers that tried to hit us.

The back story is, she met her husband while attending Edward's church in Masaka. He professed overtly to being a God-fearing Christian but lied so he could marry Annet, according to Edward. Right after the wedding, he confessed that he just wanted to possess her for his own liking.

He forced Annet to move to the village near the area of the garage church in an attempt to control her away from the Masaka church family. His plan worked well for a short time. They quickly had two children, set up a home, and nearly disappeared into the foliage. But there were physical problems starting to emerge and they were being noticed by neighbors.

"From Annet's faithful prayers the man claimed 'his things were getting spoiled'," Edward said. "He was into witchcraft and darker spiritual things. He told his wife that his worldly powers were being upset by her prayers to God Almighty, and he didn't like what was happening against his gods and against his will."

This upset her husband so badly that he beat her that afternoon, this time, he severely fractured her chest. The speculation from those who helped her right afterward claimed the injury was from the husband's foot, when he was stomping on her.

Edward caught wind of the event the next day and immediately went to the hospital where he found Annet, clinging to life. She told him her husband ran away from the village leaving the children. Edward left immediately, to find the kids and ensure their safety.

While looking for the little girl, he got further details from the neighbors. They corroborated the ongoing violence toward Annet and more history of her abusive husband. He then found Derek still at his school.

When he returned to the hospital later that evening, Annet had gotten much worse.

"Pastor how do you see me?" Annet asked in a deathly weakened voice. "Do you see me getting better?"

Edward replied in his usually hopeful spirit with a confident "Yes," to give her a bit of hope to hold onto. Hope that she wasn't alone. But whether or not he or Annet had an inkling of the final outcome, I suspect both knew what was to come. Tragically and unfairly, Annet died that evening. The fate of her children was now weighing heavily under the pastoral wings of Edward. He said later that he couldn't help feeling responsible for the damage.

Edward took both kids to his house to sleep for the night. He knew in the morning he was going to have to claim their mother's body from the hospital, but he didn't know what in the world he was going to do next. In addition to this great crisis, he too was facing personal battles.

At sunrise, after he had stopped by the hospital, Edward showed up at the door of our apartment at the compound of Brian and Angela right as I was cooking oatmeal. He was distraught. Beaten. Maudlin. Nearly incapable of making the simplest of decisions. We hugged, and then he broke apart.

"I lost my dad last year, and my mom a few years before that," his voice slumped, like his posture. "But this hurts so much worse. She was like a young daughter to me, like one of my own babies. This is so bad you know."

He continued to list the crimes of his cleric deficiencies. He was sorry he had very little money. He was sorry he couldn't pay the hospital bill. He was sorry to have to bargain with the coroner for the mother's body. He was sorry he couldn't afford to buy her a casket and instead was planning to wrap the body in tree bark cloth. He was sorry she was going to be buried in an unmarked plot in the village banana field.

"There just isn't enough pay to pay back the sacrifice of this woman. She is a martyr," he lamented.

He motioned to the passenger seat of his car. There Annet lay, reclined and covered in a dusty blanket.

There's no safety nets in Africa. There isn't a welfare system that catches innocent victims of situations like this. No official organization scoops up these newly orphaned children either. Nobody in government mends this. It's people that allow God to use them even when they don't want to, who stand in these gaps. People are afflicted without just cause everyday here. People suffer. People die.

"You know it was so severe, to me and those people whom she called family at the garage church," Edward said as he hung his head lower than I had ever seen. "Being in the mission field people expect a lot from you and to help in these times of great crisis. They expect you to know how, and what to do...but I just don't have any idea what to do right now."

Edward was also about to lose his rented house in just a few days. The pastor provider and expected leader who is supposed to have all the answers at all times to supply need, yet by his own pride, hadn't anyone to help his need. The landlord had given him barely a month's notice to get his family, livestock, and belongings down the road.

On top of that stress, he was still juggling a half a dozen churches, traveling to all of them weekly doing regular prayer meetings, trying to raise up leaders so they would become self-reliant. He was also trying to maintain the charade of being the unbroken bright spot of hope in the face of daily misery. The town's garbage was piling up too, and he was falling behind on his trash man duties. He was an essential hub to a wobbly wheel that had to keep turning, but at the same time, it was grinding away at him and about to fall off the wagon.

To him, this death had seemed like the most personal kind of failure. One that could wipe out all the good he'd been trying to keep up with.

One of the good things about living there for the extended time I did was getting familiar with the network of missionary people from different countries who were well connected in the Masaka triangle of surrounding cities. We had just shared dinner a few nights before with a young

American couple running an orphanage called Okoa Refuge a few miles down the road.

Liv and Tyler, who had shared with us over that meal, some of the most hair raising stories of traveling deep into the Congo doing rescue work that I'd ever heard firsthand. It almost made the legendary 'shotgun preacher' look like a pansy. They had barely escaped the country before a death and mugging plan was going to be executed upon them, and soon found themselves back in Africa, where their heart is, in Uganda.

The two were building their dream orphanage just outside of Masaka. They bought and developed a property to house and school nearly 60 orphans and had garnered some corporate support along the way from the U.S. They were knowledgeable about the local court system and we figured, they just might lead us to figure out what to do with these two kids. It was our only hope of developing some kind of plan for caring for Derek and Peace.

For those few hours inside our compound that morning, the two kids continued to hide behind Edward's sturdy legs, like they were peering around two pillars.

Derek gripped Peace's hand ever so tightly as Angela slowly approached, instinctively like a man protector. In the other hand he had a small pebble, the only rock solid thing he could hold onto. Peace sucked harder on that muddy thumb that had created a wet, smudgy circle around her face. A tear hung in the balance, stuck, refusing to run.

The two children fell into Angela's arms and she walked the children over to our porch, where we fed them some warm cereal. I made some for Edward and made him eat.

Brian finished up a mobile call to Liv and Tyler, who, without hesitating, said they'd take them into their facility.

Relatives and next of kin are usually called on when

kids are orphaned like this in Africa, but most times, they end up in orphanages or boarding schools becoming the burden of someone else. Or left to the streets.

We loaded us all in the van for the short trip down the valley. Derek sat on my lap. It wasn't that far, but the whole way there Edward stared out of the window of the van as we ambled down the road. Something broke inside me. I wanted to scream.

I began to process how I might get these kids out of Uganda at the same time with William. Am I a witness to this because maybe God is asking Nita and I to also carry for these as well? How long would that take? I began to mentally plot some sort of path to climbing that mountain as well.

There was this imaginary dialogue to my wife going something like, "Hey honey, I thought it would be OK if I just adopted another two kids, besides, it's cheaper by the trio when you consider it's only another couple of plane tickets." But I realized quickly once I got through my emotions, that our calling was for William and not these also. I drew Derek close to my lips and whispered a prayer into his ear.

"God is the father to the fatherless," I said. "As with Isaac who was doomed to be sacrificed and die, this God, your and my God will always supply the 'ram in the thicket', just like he did then to keep his promises."

We pulled into Okoa Refuge. The gate opened by the security man where we waded through smiles and giggles waist deep as we exited the van.

Liv took Peace and mommy clutched her to her hip. Derek followed me out, holding onto my hand. We sat down on the cement porch out of the heat surrounded by bright yellow walls painted with children caricature's dancing. The staff moms sliced up a fruit snack to break the ice.

After an hour of integrating, getting the dime tour of

their facility and letting all the changes sift, Derek took his little sister toward the playground with some of the other children and began to show us that hope was living large. He smiled and the two started to play.

Edward hadn't said a word in hours. The grass reed he'd been chewing all morning was now in his hand. A sign of what was chewing him up inside was leaving.

"My brother David," he said, "This is a great way that God has bonded us together. We are brothers, you and me now. You have come here again and now these kids are better. Their mother can now rest in peace too."

Edward's words were like those written at the battle of St. Crispins. A battle that took brave and faithful souls like that of Annet, but left behind a burning in those that survived. A burning to fight with their all because they wee among the living. That was Edward and me now.

She was more than a casualty, she was Christian martyr. Someone who laid their life down for the faith.

She was Annet Mirembe…Mirembre, the name means "peace."

Shalom Annet.

23

THE HOME STRETCH

The home stretch is when you can see the finish line coming out of the last turn. One can almost taste victory.

For us it was the phone call from the Embassy that William's immigration medical exam was ready to be scheduled. The paperwork molasses and endless setbacks to the red tape was nearing the end.

But if getting close to the home stretch had taught me anything, it was to be extra watchful of what was around and behind you. For the very thing you might ignore right next to you could take you out. Just ask a NASCAR driver.

The section right before the victory is also where the first loser would be satisfied to take everyone out of the race, just so you don't win.

Valentine's Day was approaching. William and I got another package a few days before from home. Inside were Nita's traditional heart-splashed underwear she gives me every year. Except, this time there was another package with a different pair. Those were for William.

I held up my comical silk boxers displaying them to a bewildered young boy while explaining the tradition and meaning. Then I tossed William's package over to his awaiting hands. He ripped open the paper and unfolded a pair of black boxers with a large Coca-Cola white bear holding single heart sprawled across the butt. He giggled, and blushed.

It was obvious that my wife's heart was becoming increasingly opened to include another person into our family traditions. Her heart was here. Mine was fighting daily to be somewhere else, but at the same time, it still felt needed here for a bit longer.

With that Embassy call, the thought of being home by our mid-March wedding anniversary was nearing reality, or not, depending on the last potential set-back the foreboding TB test, plus two more rides to Kampala along that wild highway, aboard public transport.

The very next morning, William and I shivered in the foggy mist as the boda-boda driver sped us to the Masaka taxi park for the first trip back.

On the two-lane Rwanda/Kampala road, there are a few, very treacherous parts, mainly one blind corner where the pot-holes are so washed out completely that the road is barely one-lane of passage. If you're following a large truck, it's good for you because he'll clear out all of the opposing traffic. But if the truck is oncoming, then it becomes a losing game of "chicken." Meaning, one of you has to dive into the pothole abyss or off the road entirely. It's never the truck.

About 90 minutes into the trip, unaware of our whereabouts, we were nearing the proximity to this notorious section of the road.

The game of "who's going to flinch first" had already been decided by the two opposing drivers. One large truck and the other was our bus. Apparently, our driver didn't get the swerve memo.

The bus suddenly and violently shifted to the left at such a degree that all hand-carried items were now airborne in slow motion. People screamed. Tires squealed. The bus tipped to the left almost to the point of no return.

"Oh my God!" someone yelled behind me.

The bus forcefully corrected its sudden zig with a huge rolling zag, and then righted itself back to center on all four wheels. A few parts of the rig sounded like they had just broken off, making that distant jiggling sound of spare parts as we left them along the roadway. My head made the last bounce off the window glass at the final lurch and forced me to look up and assess.

A screaming young college student in front of us turned around to give me her babbling play-by-play as the entire bus cried out in unison one last time.

"Did you see that? I mean did you see that truck?" the student screeched with the whites of her brown eyes taking over her dark face.

"Oh my God, we were nearly killed by that oncoming fuel truck and he didn't even pull over or stop or care," she yelled.

I shrugged, and went back to reading my book. It was the Bible, the only book I had in my pack. To the disbelief of my fellow passengers, I didn't seem to react much. Hell, we had been through so much by this time, what's one more worthless attempt to try and make us believe God wouldn't pull through? A bus wreck—is that all you got left Satan?

When you've decided to die in to keeping your word, how you go out doesn't make you panic beforehand from a close call.

We got to the Kampala clinic first in line and with some time to spare before they opened. The office was across town from the Embassy tucked in a neighborhood off the main drag about two miles from the passport office. Given the fact we were relying on Ugandan transport and the country's timetable, I call our arrival time somewhat of a miracle.

I was a bit nervous not knowing William's full medical history. Rumor had it that eighty-percent of Ugandan children have Tuberculosis (TB), which sounded disproportional, but it came from people who were running orphanages.

TB is a bacteria of the lungs spread from coughs and sneezes. With the kinds of hacking and snot lingering about Jireh at any given time, heaven only knew what William might be infected with. We were banking on a huge leap of faith that William wasn't a carrier, plus we'd just bet the bank by purchasing $4,000 worth of one-way plane tickets. If infected, it could delay us another month and cost another thousand dollars to change the flight date. We were scheduled for the following Saturday, February 23 at midnight.

We had timed the appointment so the coming weekend would be the wait time for the 72-hour incubation period. That way we could go to a local Masaka clinic to have it looked at first thing on Tuesday. Then the plan was to go back to the city with all of our luggage, finish the shots, and get the physical on the very next day, Wednesday.

The U.S. Embassy would then have the required two days to cut the visa on the Friday, just one day before our ticketed departure. We were cutting it close, but at least the math worked.

The nurse asked a hundred questions and filled out a lots of papers. She pricked William's mid-forearm and circled the needle hole with a black sharpie pen.

"If any redness or swelling goes outside of this area, we will need to treat him for TB," she explained. "I hope you have not made your departure plans yet, because many families have had to change them."

"I believe we are good on that," I said. We had already shot those dice that this wouldn't be what throws us off course.

William also needed an entire panel of youth immunizations, eight shots in total at the next visit. I could either pay for those today, or next Wednesday. And that would be another three-hundred U.S., please.

"We will square up Wednesday then," I said.

I now had to calculate how much daily cash I could extract out of the next few ATM withdrawals during the next couple of days. We needed money for the final expenses back to the city mid-week, transportation in and around the Embassy, the final airport taxi to catch the flight, lodging for two days at Hotel Triangle, food, and that little extra padding, just in case somewhere along the way we needed a "little money" for someone at a desk to wave us through.

On the bus back to Masaka that evening I leaned over to sleeping William and whispered, "we're almost home."

I wanted him to stay awake, take in all he could on this last lap into his hometown, because it I knew it would be a long while before he saw another equatorial sunset and unique beauty of his country.

I thought about his mother, Regina. All her help and appearances with the numerous court drama's, even bearing up against that verbal flogging from the Masaka judge at the guardianship hearing for being an unfit mother. I felt for her and was convicted she was owed the respect of saying goodbye to her first born.

The weekend blasted by us. Before we knew it we had said our thank yous and farewells to our dear friend Edward, the River of Life church family, to our favorite local merchants and our personal boda driver.

On Tuesday morning the black pen circle on William's arm was barely visible and there was no redness from TB. Now with a clean medical condition, and barring any freak public transport accidents, we were just days away from landing in Oregon! We hired our friend and private driver, Peter, to take us back the Kampala for the last two days before visa issue day, Friday.

The hump-day sunrise greeted us warmly as we loaded our bags into the boot of Peter's silver Mercedes. Standing there again, in the grass of Brian and Angela's in a state of awkward déjà vu'. We hugged again. Angela made sure William had his American flag, and she reminded him again what to do with it when he landed.

I spoke a few words of appreciation for them getting us through the mess of the last months, and how much we wished them well for their adoption fight for JoJo to go speedily. They told us we were an inspiration that indeed, "all things were possible." Biyinzika.

"Is this a real good bye?" I joked. "Or at the end of the day are we going to be back here asking if the apartment is still available?"

"Ain't happen-in'," Angela twanged in denial. "I already rented your unit to a group coming Monday and Edward is taking the other. You'd better be on that plane. It's the only place in your near future you'll have a place to sleep."

We tearfully said goodbye—again. William got a final kiss on the cheek from Angela.

The doors of the car closed tightly, sealing in the only air conditioning we'd felt in months. The hot, dry season wind blew the red dust away from our tires as we drove down the hill to the traffic circle. It was a walk William and I had done hundreds of times to appointments, supply runs, and mid-morning breakfast Rolexes burritos. Our previous footprints from all those trips had long disappeared, just like these last tracks from the car would be in a few moments. What lasting imprints would we leave here? More importantly, what imprints of here would leave lasting imprints on me?

We got to the clinic early from the light mid-day traffic and after briefly waiting, William received his panel of shots. I counted out the cash on the counter looking like I was placing a bet at a high stakes poker table. The nurse double-checked the file, and re-read all the test data clipped to the side. She told me she was going to have to draw the drape for a few seconds to do one last examination. Based on our mutual looks, she knew, that I knew, what was going to happen next. Turn and cough.

I swear I could see William blushing through the curtain. This was the first time parts of him were ever shown to another person. When she left the room right after, we laughed and made jokes as we cracked our first set of adolescent man fables together.

Like when I told him after arriving that America doesn't let anyone in the country with scrawny arms and unless he could do 25 push-ups. I fibbed at this golden opportunity too, saying authorities had to check his man parts to make sure they were the right dimensions to legally enter the states.

"Really?" he said almost fearfully.

"Gotcha," I smiled back.

"We're close, Bud, we're entering the home stretch." I assured him. "We lived through the courts, the Homeland Security and the adoption paperwork, through the pain, tears, joy, and the duties of obedience that God has put before us. We've even lived through the dry season. Not just here with the weather, but through the days where we didn't think we would get here. And now, we're here."

The last thing left was for the Homeland electronic adoption file to be uploaded to the Embassy dropbox—the last item on the checklist that all of the legalities were done back home and from here.

There were ironclad assurances through Chris at the senator's office that the file would be uploaded in the next 24 hours. She was tracking it like a starving hunter after a bear. This allowed us plenty of time for the Kampala office with the time change, to grant and stamp William's passport Visa during their normal Friday business hours.

Then again, the home stretch isn't a guarantee. One crash can take out the leader and many others.

And then suddenly, the losers become the winners.

We were on track to win all right, but just exactly "how" would become the stuff of family lore.

24

THE SNOWSTORM FROM HELL

The few days prior to our medical exam Nita had gotten news that our Homeland Security file was missing. Again. This was the second time, I didn't tell William.

He had told me just hours before that call, "Dad, I think we are down to the final half-finger."

"What do you mean?"

"Well they've pretty much cut off all the others and I feel we are down to the final stub," he joked. "I feel our departure is very close, even within the week."

Briefly hopeful and briefly horrified, I was chewing on that last stub's fingernail during William's medical exam and shot series that there would be good news of the missing file. Nita hadn't heard the whereabouts of it for more than 24 hours, and now we were at the last possible day the visa could be issued before our flights.

I continued to further the charade that all was well, because in reality, we couldn't do anything but continue on in this final faith march. God's people were continuing to confirm our departure. Details on our end were still going through. The file would show up, eventually. Besides, our plane tickets—$4400—were non-refundable. This was the blitz to the finish. We had to finish.

Nita and Chris were calling each other at least twice a day. The senate secretary was hunting through all her up-line official contacts to keep the dogs sniffing out our file in the mass pile of bureaucratic bowel.

Early Wednesday evening, Thursday morning our time, Chris received an e-mail that the file had been located and was next up on the docket to be entered into the system. That meant it should arrive at the embassy just in the nick of time.

I asked Nita to forward me copies of those e-mails to the Hotel Triangle so I could add them to my book of paperwork—just in case.

Everything I had collected over the course of these last months was bulging in a green plastic expandable file I kept under my arm like the White House nuclear code football. There were at least six copies deep of everything proving William was ours and authorizing me to take him out of the country. This book-sized dossier with a bungee wrapped around it was never out of my backpack, which was never off my body, which was never out of my sight.

I believe it even saved our bacon when we got stopped at a surreptitious police checkpoint while riding a rented motorcycle to see Lake Victoria in that final week of our last African bike adventures.

The famous lake was only 15 miles or so away due East from our apartment. There was a missionary we had met at River of Life church who had a witchcraft rescue operation on Bugala Island. He shared some hair-raising stories of what he encountered there and said we had an open invitation to visit anytime. Sure, I was curious.

William had never been in on the island, much less on a boat ferry before, so we rented a motorcycle from our favorite boda driver and took off to the village port of Bukakata to catch the transport across the lake channel.

Bombing down the dirt rode that afternoon without a care in the world, wind through our hair and dust in our teeth, we came across a young woman carrying a baby and looking weary.

After stopping, William spoke to her. She said she was on her way to the ferry boat and had been walking for much of the day, but was concerned she wasn't going to make it there in time for one of its four departures that day. She looked dehydrated and the baby had dust matted to his little face. I reached in my pack and gave her a bottle of water to which she thanked us profusely.

We squeezed her and the baby onto the back of our two-person seat, joking about our new business of being country Boda-boda taxi drivers. I teasingly asked William how much we should charge her for the trip, because this was easy money picking up people along the road. Like the local drivers, I moved way forward to ride on the tank, and steered with my thighs.

About three miles from the lake ramp was a barren stretch. Up ahead I spotted a potentially unnerving situation. Four uniformed policemen, lounging in the shade along the roadside berm, dressed in white, bloused combat boots, AK-47 rifles at their sides. They stood abruptly as they spotted us coming.

One man stepped out in the roadway and put the hand not carrying the rifle up in the air. The others stood watch and fanned out in a semi-circular formation around us when we stopped. I felt it best to keep the bike running.

After the broken-English greetings the officer asked why I was operating a taxi this far from the city. I explained that we rented the bike for the day and were only giving a ride to someone in need to catch the same ferry.

He asked to see my driver's license. Then my passport. Then my international driver's license. Each time he checked a document, he looked over to who I assumed was the boss of the platoon. I'm certain they were looking for some sort of bribe, or a legal offense they could stick on us, but thanks to the thick green file, I had all the paperwork they asked for.

Finally the boss pointed to his head.

"How come you are not wearing a helmet?" the officer said from the prompting.

"Helmet?" I quizzed.

"Yes, we have a helmet law in Uganda," he said with a poker smile.

"Well, you'd better tell the 40,000 boda drivers in the province behind us because I don't think anyone's gotten that word out yet," I said.

They all laughed. One of those sinister kind of laughs you hear in a movie just before everyone gets shot. The officer in front of us laughed again and then shouted through the shade of his ball cap, "You are a very funny Muzungoo!"

He theatrically stepped aside, bowing slightly with his hand extended as if to introduce us to the roadway ahead. He then waved us through the check point.

Meanwhile, back home and after days of uncertainty, our adoption file finally surfaced on someone's desk in the Midwest. The Homeland Security part of the file had to go from an office in the Midwest, then hard copies needed to be sent somewhere on the East Coast to be electronically scanned and uploaded to the embassy and in Kampala's dropbox.

Chris had traced the whereabouts and sent e-mails to all of the up-line recipients to keep it moving swiftly and meet our departure deadline. She had just sent us confirmation that it was on the way. Just to make sure William and I were on the high-alert priority, I'd called the Embassy and spoken to the manager, the woman who had walked us through the process since our first denial. Though we started off on the wrong foot, we were at least working together by this time. She diplomatically and cautiously confirmed our visa appointment for the next morning at 10 a.m., though with a procedural caveat.

"Mr. Loveall, we still have you scheduled to receive the visa for William, but I must tell you, if we do not receive the electronic file from the U.S., we cannot process your request. I suspect we should be getting it at any moment, but I just wanted to let you know, my hands are tied unless I get that."

I told her of my e-mail confirmations, with verifying copies, but she was sticking to her original statement. No file. No visa.

Though I had nibbled off the last bit of substance from my nails, I was still confident all was going to be OK, barring of course, some freak *euroclydon*, a freak swirling storm, blowing in from nowhere.

The way I had it figured, we still had an entire afternoon to spare while the waking business day in the states was commuting to work.

I had specific orders from Nita as to what William was going to wear off the plane. It was an outfit that looked like he was a member of the USA Olympic team. A red white and blue athletic top, styling jeans, Nike logos on his feet. Only thing left then, was to get his hair done.

Since this time, William had never had any hair before. For his whole life, it was buzz shaved like the rest of the young boys and men of Uganda. In fact, as I was letting his hair grow out, preparing his head for the winter arrival back home, a great many strangers on the street would stop us and point fingers at me for the length of his hair.

"Hey, why don't you cut this boy's hair?" they would say. "He looks like a drug dealer."

After a guy in a salon shaped Williams' hair to his liking, we went a few doors down to the American café for the most authentic hamburger, fries and a real ice cream milkshake on the continent. I told William this is 'Americana' on a plate, with pizza being the only food that would beat it.

"What's a pizza like?" William asked, as he bit into the closest taste of America in Africa.

"It's the near perfect food," I said dreaming and salivating. "It's slices of cheese, meat and saucy splendor that is your mom and my favorite. My bet, William, is that it will become yours, too."

At the other end of the mall where this American style café was, blinked a lit sign to a six-lane bowling alley.

"You know what a bucket list is William?" I asked as I paid the check to the waiter. He shook his head. After a short explanation I said, "It's doing something, somewhere, that you can't do anywhere else. Most opportunities come when you have to make quick decisions to do them. Like right now."

"I've never did bowling before," he said looking anxiously over toward the sign.

"Until today!" I said. We stood up from the table and heading across the parking lot to the other end of mall. "Your mom can't get past the idea of wearing someone else's shoes, that's why we don't do bowling back home, so I'm hoping the shoe thing won't bother you."

I doubt he really knew what I was talking about but it didn't matter. Come to find out, in Uganda, bowling shoes don't even exist. You bowl in your socks. It was as if we were sliding on bare ice coming up to the foul line to throw, making it more difficult to get a good line on knocking down the pins. The approach got slicker and more challenging as the game wore on, and our scores reflected this deviation.

Back on the other side of the planet, Nita had been monitoring a potential new deviation of her own. A snow storm had been moving like an icy tsunami across the Midwest for the past 24 hours. By the time her Wednesday day-off was coming to a close, she had gotten several calls from Chris who had given her varying updates of "good news, bad news."

"The good news is, your files are very next in line to be uploaded to the Homeland Security office in Rhode

Island and it's on desk of the person I've been in direct contacted with," she said. "The bad news is, the snow storm is so bad that none of the employees at the Chicago office could get to work today to get that done."

The last blast of winter had nearly shut down the whole mid-region of the U.S. Our "everything-is-in-order" afternoon lunch and bowling turned extremely tense and uncertain. Nita and Chris had exhausted every line of help during that Wednesday shut-down, because it was by now, well into business Thursday in Uganda.

We were down to the very, very last possible hours for the file to meet the Embassy's required timing for our Friday issue. We went back to the hotel and nervously waited through dinner, then watched some TV. Around midnight, William went to sleep watching me pace and sigh.

By then, I had pretty much fussed my way through Nita's sleep cycle and she was dragging herself to work Thursday morning. We spoke just before she left and in a few hours, she and Chris would have a chance to see how the storm was going to treat us either with good news or freeze us with bad.

The further problem was that the storm was rapidly heading toward the Eastern seaboard and those people, to beat the onset, were already starting to leave work early. This was going to delay their ability to upload the file even if they got it in the next few hours. A normal, stateside Thursday workday was not looking hopeful. I was beginning to think we didn't have an ice-cubes chance in Hell of pulling this off, barring some snow-plow type miracle.

Just after her lunch time Nita called and hung up, waking me out of a stress-dream coma around 3 a.m. This was the signal for me to call back when she had news if the file had been uploaded. Apparently, I'd fallen asleep with not only the phone in my hand, but fully clothed on the floor of the hotel room while praying for our happy ending I called. "Chris said that she called a supervisor back in Minnesota last night and told him our story," said Nita. "He was so moved by it that he fought his way back into the city through the storm for us. He was one of only five other employees in the whole government building that made it into work today. They found the file in the electronic system, and he said he uploaded it late this afternoon to two different federal addresses and also the Ugandan Embassy."

She paused. Did this mean what I thought it did? "I think we got our miracle," she said.

My countenance was pretty shot by then. All the ups and downs had stripped me of any filters. Even though this was good news, it came again at the expense of withdrawal of emotional stress.

"Who the hell writes this kind of crap?" I vented, partially in relief, but mostly in disbelief. It was really a masked statement of happiness, but was wrapped and warped from marching around the same mountain of frustration and setback for so long.

We consoled each other's emotions for a few minutes, but suddenly my phone cut out. I was out of airtime. It was now 3:45 in the morning. Where does a guy buy an airtime scratch-it scrip at this time of the night—in Uganda?

Early the next morning, after a failed attempt to get one from the hotel's night clerk, I scored an airtime card from a street vendor. Then it was show time at the U.S. Embassy, the come-back-again-when-you-jump-through-these-ten-hoops moment.

Though our appointment wasn't until 10 a.m., I planned to head off any new disasters by getting there at 8 a.m. when the doors first open. Either to plea with the officials, pry open a computer terminal, or get someone on my phone stateside who could vouch for my claims.

After a cab ride to the Embassy, the guards at the gate waved us through. By now, we were regulars and the guy logging personal items into the lockers even remembered my last name.

"Mr. Loveall are we going to be seeing you again? Or is this the last?"

"Hopefully Joseph, this is the last stop on a very difficult journey."

"May God grant you what you two are requesting then," he said.

"Ameena." It means amen.

Word passed that we were waiting, which may have gotten someone to look again at the computer uploads as their first task of the work day. The U.S. workday was now night. If it didn't get done in those last few hours, it wasn't going to happen for another week.

We waited for two hours. Room 3 opened up. The same room where our first rejection took place. A familiar pit settled uneasily in my stomach.

We were called in and the same supervisor sat down with only a single piece of paper in her hand. Perhaps for a final signature of some sort before we celebrated and high-tailed it out of there.

"I'm sorry," she said.

I couldn't be hearing this, could I?

"As you can see Mr. Loveall, I am bound by these set of rules and regulations before I can grant anyone a visa."

I whipped out a copy of the e-mail from the senator's officer verifying the existence of the uploaded electronic adoption folder. But, before I could say another word she barreled through her scripted agenda.

"We are supposed to have hard copies of the files to really be fully authorized to grant a visa. I was promising to do you a favor by allowing the electronic ones to serve for now, while we waited for the hard copy package. Although you have a copy of an e-mail someone supposedly sent me, the file is not in where it's supposed to be. Unless something happens by the end of our work day, today, I'm afraid we will have to work this out at another time."

Maybe the miracle of that moment was civility. Because by that time, irritation and disappointment were so far down the list of feelings that the only shred of emotion I could muster was gratitude.

"I thank you then for all you've done so far," I said, packing up my green folder. "We are staying in Kampala until this is over. Would you please call me if anything changes that would put us on our midnight flight we have seats for tomorrow?"

"I certainly will. Again, I'm very sorry. I know you've worked really hard."

I smiled back at her.

The sky was turning black with storm clouds and the wind was picking up by the time we got back onto the street. We sauntered down the hill to a café that served ice cream. Rain started to spit. That familiar smell of water on hot pavement reminded me of home.

We stood vigil at the roadside table for the rest of the day. Every so often one of us would say to the other something like, "God's going to come through, because He knows we don't have any other place to go."

I found myself thinking of all the people involved in this story. Pastors, lawyers, family, friends, churches, Facebook friends, , judges, local missionaries, Brian and Angela, Bob and Mary, and William's mother Regina.

Suddenly, my cell phone rang. It was 4:30 p.m. The caller ID read, "Embassy."

"Mr. Loveall?" It was that familiar voice of the visa woman.

"Yes."

"I'm sorry, but we've not gotten anything yet from the United States that has shown up in our system or the shared electronic dropbox."

"O.K." I said.

"Are you aware that there is a severe snow storm that has pretty much shut done the whole East Coast in the last 48 hours.

"Yes, we are more than aware. In fact, my people tell me a government guy in Minnesota drove back into town and e-mailed the file, hoping you'd get it in time. And we're all scratching our heads out here, not sure why you don't have it in the form you need it or in some e-mail server."

"Well, this is what I'm willing to do for you, Mr. Loveall. I have to come in here on Saturdays to check security alerts on my e-mail between 8 a.m. and 10 a.m. I will also check for the file and if, and if it is here, I will issue your visa. Can you be near here at 10 a.m. to meet me out front within a few minutes if that happens? I say that because you can't be waiting in front of the building at all when we are closed."

I burst out laughing. A woman who I had decided was against us all along, was now going above and beyond to render aid.

"We will be waiting at the café just to the west of you," I said.

"Good. I will be calling you by 10 a.m. That will give the states their entire Friday workday to get the right file in the place where I can access it. I will let you know then, what I am able to do, if anything."

"Wow. I can't believe you would do that for us. Thank you, thank you very much."

There was a definite spirit moving in those final hours, even with everything still dangling in the balance. The best way to describe what was going on is that a spirit of closure was marching on, even if the evidence and e-mail files were lagging behind. There was also a peace in me holding down the potential panic that wanted to run rampant with the final seconds ticking down.

With just over twenty-four hours before the plane we had tickets for was leaving, one fact remained, it hadn't left without us.

At least not yet anyway.

25

THE LAST GOODBYES

Staring at potentially our final hours in Africa, I thought again of William's mother, Regina. I owed her at least a last goodbye from her firstborn.

Before we left our watch at the café down the street from the Embassy that evening, I called in hopes of arranging a final meeting with her and her first born. This could, quite possibly, be our final night in Africa. I didn't want to regret missing this opportunity.

"Yes! Yes!" she said, in her small amount of English words after I finally made a phone connection. Apparently, she was out visiting a cousin and was close by. We made arrangements to meet where she was, near a marketplace a few streets below the hotel.

When we met up, the first thing she said to William was that someone had told her we had already gone and she had been very sad the last couple of days.

She hadn't eaten all day so we walked back up to the main drag for some chicken and chips. Regina talked up a storm over dinner, laughing, engaged, wanting to make that final connection with William.

As I watched the two of them it was obvious they had a connection, but it wasn't the mother/son bond that I suspected Regina might have hoped for. Sadly, it was more a conversation between curious acquaintances, living continents apart, one going on the voyage of a lifetime, the other trying to grasp its enormity while watching from shore.

If we were to count the times they spent together over the past eight years since she dropped him off at the grandparents hut, they were few. Marrying a Muslim man who wanted her, but not her boy, forced a gut-wrenching decision by her. Regrettably, the choices of survival dictate such actions. The way William frames it in his own mind was, his mother was poor, and not able to care for him. Then his grandparents were poor and unable. Finally, the aunt was poor and unable. Nobody with enough—let's face it—money.

I'm not trying to be judgmental or point blame. The real crime here was the poverty of self-survival stripping the intimate family connection from a young boy who had no control over the matters.

Like any mother, I believe Regina wanted the best for William. In these last months she fought hard with us to gain what I know she couldn't provide. It was an opportunity to right whatever wrongs she thought still counted against her.

Now, this was it. The last moments were about to unfold. Regina started to give me a quick hug, but I sensed it was to avoid eye contact and the possible emotion that would follow. I took her hands and looked right into her deep brown and beautiful eyes. All the previous times I'd looked here, I'd seen joy, gratitude and humility. Now, I saw a glaze of tender ache.

"Nita and I will take good care of him," I said.

She nodded and then tried to look away in embarrassment, but I pulled her damp face gently close to mine.

"We will love him dearly, and train him be the man God has called him to be. I promise you that."

Regina was facing away from William as he spoke back my words, interpreting every last word from me. A tear streamed down her wheat bread face. She wiped it quickly, I assumed so William wouldn't notice.

"You are a very strong woman. God will bless you for the sacrifice you are making for William." She nodded even before William finished the sentence.

One of the boda-drivers pulled very close to take her home. She slipped onto the seat side-saddle. I stepped to the opposite side of the bike to pay the driver and to give William a chance to step in, and to say, or do something toward his birth mother one final time.

The driver and I confirmed the destination. I glanced up. To my surprise, William was already on the other boda-taxi, some 10 feet away, ready to go. As if right on cue, a thundercloud lit up over the gloomy hills to the North, sending a clap across the damp and dirt mudded streets. The driver of Regina's boda opened the throttle and took off.

Regina waved a few fingers longingly in his direction. William was talking to the boda driver, negotiating fare, explaining directions back to the hotel.

He never looked over at his mom, and never looked back to watch her leave. His mother, never took her eyes off of him. I waited until the last possible second for him to make final notice of her.

And just before she crested a hill a few blocks away, I put my hand up over my head, waving goodbye. She disappeared behind a small red tail light.

Back at the hotel, I phoned Nita with the news of our last-ditch Saturday chance. She was facing another emotional uphill Friday and I was looking at another edgy sleepless night. There were only eight hours of U.S. workday, to find a way, to find the file, to find a way to get on that plane.

What we didn't know at the time, was that the file uploading process was two-fold upload. The brave-the-storm guy in Minnesota had sent it to the guy in Rhode Island. He was then supposed to send it to the Embassy.

The snowstorm was now rolling into the Eastern cities, shutting down work and sending people home. Nita phoned Chris as early as she thought appropriate, and Chris, bless her heart, went right into the office early Friday to light some fires.

"I was watching Good Morning America in disbelief," Nita said, looking back. "After all of the hurdles we'd cleared thus far, to be knocked out at the end by a freak of nature was blowing my mind."

"Chris and I were doing again the whole good news-bad news exchanges throughout the morning. We both were on pins and needles for much of the day. She would call a place, nobody would be in the office or somehow the file would be really hard to find. One time the entire computer system shut down and it couldn't be transmitted because they were in the restart phase."

Nita gave me updates a few times during the night and well into my Saturday morning. Good news. Bad news. Then, at 4 a.m., possible good news.

"David, Chris just called me and she assures me the file was found by someone who said it looked complete and was uploaded by the Rhode Island office. It's now into the U.S. Embassy system," she said. "It all should be there at least a few hours before the supervisor lady gets in."

"Unbelievable." I said sarcastically. "It's like a bad movie with too many plot twists for the sake of drama. For what reason? There weren't enough car chases to make it exciting? What could possibly happen next to top this?"

In retrospect, we both agreed, it was to make sure all our personal efforts were set aside, weak works in comparison to the grand works of God. He wanted to be made known. It was also to confirm that the most difficult fight of our lives was worth it, and it was going be in His will for His glory—not in ours for our glory.

I wrote on Facebook that morning: "We Jesus followers always joke and preach about 'the eleventh hour God' working in our lives, but none of us want to ever go past 10:30! I couldn't believe the news. This is good. And this is definitely God just a few seconds before midnight!"

Nita fidgeted into her evening hours as we were eating our eggs at our breakfast time like sleep-deprived zombies. Cutting through the lobby to catch a boda over to a closed Embassy Saturday morning, I arranged a late checkout with the desk clerk for 5 p.m. Our plane was leaving at midnight, and I was hopeful William and I would be on it, even if stowed in cargo space.

Out by the curb we found our go-to taxi driver.

"We are leaving today my friend," I said. "Would it be possible to leave here around 4:30 to beat some of the traffic to the airport?"

"Even if I must cancel a customer, I will wait for you," he said.

"Wonderful."

The motorcycle taxi dropped us right in front of the café. We sat at our usual table across the street from the Embassy, for yet another stakeout. I looked at my watch, 7:55 a.m. The way I had it figured, we should be back on a boda headed toward the hotel in two hours, max.

An hour went by.

Then two.

I figured the visa supervisor slept in a bit and there was nothing to be nervous about. Nita called and hung up, and I called her a few minutes after 10 a.m.

"Nothing yet," I said.

"What? Really? Is she even there?"

"All I know and trust is that she said she would be there, but I haven't heard a thing since yesterday. I've had my eyes locked on the entrance the whole time I've been here, but I can't tell really if anyone's gone in. But no one has come out either."

My insides were weaving themselves into a huge ball of anguish. I could barely talk. I wanted to storm the gates and claim what was ours.

"Honey, all we can do is wait. And I can wait up until about 8 p.m. That's when I figure the fat lady solos."

"Dad, how long are we going to wait here?" asked William, slumping lower into the steel patio chair.

"Until my phone rings, or until this café place closes tonight, my boy," I said. "I believe somehow, some way, we are going to be on that plane tonight."

I counted every car that drove by our stakeout and watched it pass by the Embassy. Still nobody in. Nobody out. The guards stood their vigil idly and with little movement.

The chrome plastic casing on my mobile phone vibrated sharply on the metal table top. With cat-like reflexes I plucked the phone off the surface. William perked to attention. The street noises mysteriously ceased. For the next precious moments everything in the world hung in the balance of the next utterances through that mobile device.

"Mr. Loveall," the Embassy woman said, "can you come to the front of the building now?"

"I will be there before you will."

I turned to William. "Let's roll!"

We dashed up the hill along the grass and the beaten path to the guarded driveway. With our hasty zeal, we startled the gate guard. He momentarily grasped his weapon suddenly by its barrel near his hip but then swung it to the rear when he recognized who we were.

"Sorry we were running," I said. "We're just making sure we don't miss our appointment with the embassy supervisor."

The guard looked baffled, but before he could tell

us the Embassy was closed for the weekend, a woman with a packet opened the secure door and stepped into the mid-morning sunshine.

"Mr. Loveall?," It was her, the Embassy woman whose face and voice I knew well by now. "My name is Laura, and I have finally secured your visa for William." She turned to my son. "And William, it's nice to finally meet you with this good news."

She went on to explain the kind of morning she had. Her two kids had been up sick all night, which made her late getting into the office exactly at 8 a.m. as she had promised. She apologized for taking so long to finally call us. I looked at my watch, it was nearly 2pm.

"I must admit, I did do something I wasn't really supposed to do, but I knew you had a flight to catch this evening," she said. "When I got into the office and checked the computer, I saw that, indeed, the file had been uploaded, but only partially and fragmented in a couple of different places.

"Also the security code that goes with the file, which gives us access to the locked information was truncated. So even if I wanted to download the portions of the file that were there, I couldn't get past the security system's lock."

Her hands were grasping a sealed manila envelope with a Ugandan passport on top of it. Based on her warm smile and demeanor, I sensed that was our grail.

"It took me a few hours to try a number of 'back door' attempts to hack into the system and get the necessary documentation to issue William's visa, but I was able and I've got it right here."

"So you've been playing James Bond with the Embassy computer system on a Saturday morning just to help us?" I said. "I'm so thankful, but why would you do that?"

"This assignment in Uganda is very difficult," she

said. "I see many families like you who come here to give orphan kids a life, a chance, love—and all they face is red tape, hardship and great sacrifices. Many of them quit and end up leaving the kids worse off then when they started."

"I have two daughters. Living here is hard for my whole family. If I can show anything to my girls it would be to see the suffering of other people as an opportunity to do something good. Also, to not lose heart during the process when things go wrong. It's been a tough lesson for me, but you Mr. Loveall, you and your family fought hard for William, and I know this will be a great blessing for him and your family."

Not only was I still reeling from the details of what she had done for us, but I was still stuck on the fact that this was a former adversary known only as the "Embassy Lady".

Now, I realized, she had a name, Laura. And a family. And, above all, a heart.

"I don't know what to say, Ms. Laura. Yes, you're right, it was extremely hard to battle through all this. You can't imagine the kinds of opposition we have faced not only financially, emotionally, and spiritually too. There were many times I wanted to give up, but I couldn't. Many times I feared we would never get to this day."

She smiled warmly in front of me, much like the sun that was shining itself on my back.

"So William, here is your passport. And if you look right here," she said.

She pulled the passport away from the manila envelope and turned to the page with the colorful page glued in. "This is what is going to allow you entry to your new home. I am happy to be a part of getting you there."

She turned to me. "This is the printed file of entry. It is sealed in this envelope and can only be opened by the clerk at your port of entry. Do not, under any circumstances, let anyone else tell you they need to look at what's inside or open this before you get to Portland."

She patted the packet sandwiched between her palms. I noticed the back of her hands, a tell-tale sign of a woman's age, and based on what I saw, she couldn't have been more than mid-thirties.

"I wish you both well." She stepped toward William and gave him a hug and then turned toward me. I didn't know if I was going to jump up in her arms and knock her down or settle for a dignified hand shake and be about our business. The moment was briefly uncomfortable but after all I'd been through, there wasn't much of a filter left in me.

She got the overly-appreciative hug, both arms, double squeeze. *Boo-ya!*

"Well, I've got a few appointments with my family this afternoon," she said, seemingly a bit embarrassed—if also thrilled—at my embrace. She straightened her collared shirt over her shorts, cleared her throat and took a step back toward the secure entrance door.

"Thank you again, Laura." I said waving the sealed packet at her. She waved shyly and closed herself back into the building.

William and I stood there for a few moments, astounded. He was looking at his visa picture now affixed into his own passport. The one we laughed while the photo was being taken because the photographer had to put wads of paper behind William's ears so they would show prominently in the direct, face on, pose.

I pulled my mobile phone out of my backpack pocket and punched in Nita's number. I knew she wasn't sleeping as it was nearly midnight her time.

"Our God is an 11:59-hour God," I said. "We have a visa and a sealed immigration packet and we are heading to the hotel to check out and then to the airport."

There was a pause and an emotional exhale on both sides of the phone.

"We're coming home, babe. William and I are coming home."

I could hear Nita crying on the other end of the phone. Weariness and snow storms and uncertainty and no sleep had emptied both of us over the last two nights.

"In another day and a half of travel time we will be in Eugene," I said. "We did it babe, we endured, and fought, and trusted God, and because of these last second miracles, we're going to make that flight tonight. There's nothing that can stop us now."

"Still, please be careful and get home," she said. "At least now I can get some sleep, that's after I call all of our friends and relatives of course. I can't wait to see you. I love you!"

"You'd better love me forever after all of this!" I said.

After hanging up with Nita, we took a few photos alongside the road with William holding up his passport. We boda'd back to the hotel and I began to lay out the plan for the trip home. First was to grab a shower as we weren't going to be getting one until after we landed in America.

I got on line quickly and posted this on Facebook: "All of you who prayed and interceded, give yourself a "Hallelujah." Write this in your prayer journals that God moves on behalf of his people, just when their faith is brought to the brink of weakness and rupture. He rushes to redeem, restore, and reveal."

Which was quickly followed by Nita's post:

"It is now well after midnight in the USA. We have been running the last leg of the race all day. Now standing before the finish line and ...waiting...waiting...and...David just called...WE HAVE A VISA!!!! My boys are coming home!!!

Praise You Lord Jesus!!!! The enemy kept the fight to the absolute last minute and IN JESUS NAME WE HAVE VICTORY..."

And then Mikayla: “IT'S OFFICIAL!!!! William has a visa for the USA, I have a new little brother who I can't wait to see, and I get to see my dad finally after nearly 3 months!!! Sunday at 3:16 p.m. can't come fast enough!!! Can't wait for the whole family to be home together!!”

The final domino to the story had fallen. We had the visa affixed in William’s passport to get him out of Uganda and we had time to still catch our plane. We had a green expandable file six deep of official copies. Guardianship documents, stamped letters, court orders, and now a sealed immigration packet for entry back into the U.S.

After three months of battle there was nothing I could think of that could stop us now.

So I thought.

26

POWER PLAY AND SWORDS

Emotions and anticipation were running high for a change. After we showered and rolled our bags to the curb, we found our faithful taxi driver waiting outside just as he had promised. It was as if the flood gates of cooperation were finally opening after being dammed for so long.

I asked the driver if he had eaten anything. Naturally, he hadn't. There was a great American-style restaurant right outside the airport gates with a large deck overlooking Lake Victoria, where I told him to take us first. We had the rest of the afternoon to blow before the airport opened to take the passengers for the night flights.

"Please, celebrate with us and be our guest for dinner."

The driver nodded enthusiastically, and, after the 40-kilometer trip, joined us for the celebratory feast: steak and Cokes.

The terminal check-in wasn't opened for another three hours, but the excitement of getting inside the departure area and settling in with packed bags on a cart for a one-way trip was more than magical for William. The last time he'd been there was when I told him I wouldn't leave without him. And we finally find ourselves ready and waiting in the outer snack bar, with nothing in our way of leaving.

Around 7 p.m., just as darkness settled in, we changed into long pants and short-sleeved shirts for the overnight flight to Amsterdam. Once we finished our transition and right before we were allowed to wheel our bags through the security area, we called Nita with some of the last few minutes we had left on our mobile phone. Surprisingly, she was awake at 5:30am her time, still tossing and turning in anticipation of possible snag in the works. Let's face it, amid some burst of wonder, that had been the default format.

William asked her how he was supposed to sleep on the plane and how long it would be until he would see her.

"It's just one more day away," she said. "I love you!"

"I love you too!"

Three bags, two stuffed with native handmade purses for a fund-raiser and the other with our combined assets were checked onto the black conveyer belt beside the pretty woman with the welcoming smile. KLM airlines now had our bags. I had William. We both had our carry-on packs. In mine was my final change of clothes, my Bible, our passports, the sealed packet, and the bullet-proof green file with papers in triple triplicate that were going to get us out of Africa.

Around the corner from where our bags were dropped and boarding passes issued was the last stop before our fly-away to America. Customs.

When I had filled out the card and stepped up to the desk where the brown uniformed officer sat, I noticed we were the only two people in the passageway. Strange that with all of the boarding bustle and hundreds of departing passengers, we would be so isolated.

"Passports," the officer said with a dull tone.

I handed him my passport first, then William's Ugandan passport already opened to the visa page. I figured that would simplify any immediate questions he might have.

He looked over the passports. He typed something on his computer screen. He then took our passports and slid them under his arm and out of reach.

"Where do you think you're taking this boy?" he asked with the scowl of a detective.

"Home," I said. "He's with me. He's *mine*."

"You're not taking any one of mine out of this country," he said glancing away back at the monitor.

For a fleeting instant I thought he was just badgering me. Bad joke. Late night boredom breaker. He then shot back a very serious glance, and waited for my response.

"Oh, yes I am!" I said. Then I slid my pack back off my shoulder and thumped it right in front of him. If this guy wants to play poker, or chicken, count me in.

"What do you want to see? I have full legal right to walk on that plane with this young man and I've got any documentation you need to see!"

He listed off nearly every shred of documentation I had. Legal Guardianship, relatives letter, Court Orders, the works.

"And they all better have the certification stamp or I won't accept them," he said with a combative stare.

One by one I stacked the deck in front of him. He grumbled and quipped back at me with comments in Ugandan.

"Let me see your immigration packet."

He motioned to the sealed manila envelope I had locked in my left hand. Hesitantly, I handed it over. He rolled over to his hip to unsheathe pocket knife clipped to his belt.

"I'm going to have to open this to make sure you have the right to take this boy out of my country," he said, flipping the packet out over to the taped seam at one end.

That fight-or-flight thing must have kicked in. That packet wasn't so much our ticket to get out of Africa, it was the only way I was going to get him into America. No airport security flunky was going to be the sniper to bring the final leg of this mission down.

"Listen, I don't know who you think you are—." My bravado scared me; it was as if I was speaking on heart-powered instincts. But once I started, there was no stopping.

"You know as well as I do that you're not authorized to open that packet and don't you *dare* break that seal. I've given you all the documents you need to let us pass and if you have a problem with any of this, I'll call for your superiors to help us out, I'm sure they will understand what's going on here. Am I clear? So, are we are finished here?"

He shuffled and stacked the papers I had given him on top of the sealed file and placed the passports on top. I figured he was folding and the game was over, but he bluffed with his weak pair of deuces one last time.

"I need to see a certified copy of your passport."

"That's crap and you know it! You have my original passport right there in your hands!" I yelled back. "You don't need to see anything else."

"If you can't produce that, I will direct you to secondary screening. Right now there isn't anyone available to screen you until after your flight leaves," he said with a power-trip smirk across his face.

Confident I'd have a copy left in the green folder, I rifled through the pockets. *Oh, no.* I had given the last one to the Embassy for the final visa. I didn't have another certified copy of my passport left. He wanted another color copy with an official stamp by a Notary on it. They're supposed to be an equally authorized representation of the passport that gets stapled to official paperwork or, on the off chance, serve as a substitute piece of ID if you find yourself caught in a jam.

Mentally, I was checking every pocket within a 20-foot radius, when suddenly a vision of a passport copy came to mind. My insulin blood-test kit. I had one in there.

On the previous trip with Nita, we had made certified copies of our passports and placed them in pockets we were sure to have on us at any given time. My insulin was sure to be with us always.

I dug through my carry-on clothes and unzipped my injection kit finding a half folded, worn and blood test-stained copy. With the official blue stamp still legible.

Laying down the final hand, like a royal flush, I unfolded the paper in front of him.

"I believe we are done here," I said firmly taking from him the stack of proof documents the agent was holding between us.

I grabbed William and started walking toward the gift shop and toward the gate. Within a few yards we rounded the corner through the gift shop and down to the snack bar. No one in pursuit and no obstacles ahead. But I wasn't relaxed anymore by any means. It was like a bad case of PTSD flashbacks kicking in.

The clock read just after 8:30. There were two more hours before the airplane wheels left the ground and I could breathe that final sigh of relief

An hour before boarding I made one final call to Nita, telling her of our "near miss" with the customs desk.

Midway through the brief "I love you's," my phone succumbed to pay-as-you-go minutes, and died. Fitting. Our Africa journey was over. People were now de-boarding off the very plane through the terminal that was turning back to Amsterdam. It was time to go through the gate security and into the jet-way waiting area.

The night flight routine had begun and we blended seamlessly into the few hundred passengers and mixed-race travelers. Our boarding passes had the red dot which means we were first through the stairs and onto the dimly lit tarmac.

The noise of the plane's auxiliary power engines hummed loudly. My walk slowed as I took in the final moments. Looking back at the orange-lit airport, feeling the warm tropical breeze off the lake, and smelling the familiar burning of debris, I felt like a piece of me was forever pinned here. A part of me that I never thought I'd be willing to leave. A part that I could never take back either.

I realized I had a heart for Africa. Like Edward said, "You are a father to Africa now. You have taken into your care one of ours and because of that, you are now part of us."

I walked just outside of the flow from which the main stream of people were filing toward the exterior staircase at the rear of the plane.

"I'm leaving these swords," I said aloud as if to shake hands with a parting comrade. It was a final goodbye to all of the spiritual guardians of God who had helped fight this lengthy battle. Those two swords, one of warriorship and the other of God's truth, were stuck into the ground when I arrived. Those same two, I thought would be picked up again when leaving to place at the next outpost, I instead decided to leave.

They'll be needed again, I thought. This is a place to which I must return.

"Come on, Dad, let's go," William said.

"And where are we going?" I said jokingly. "After all of this, where do we go from here?"

"Let's go home, Dad," he said quietly.

And, this time, we did.

27

HOME AT THE BREAKFAST TABLE

"God decided in advance to adopt us into his own family by bringing us to himself through Jesus Christ. This is what he wanted to do, and it gave him great pleasure." **Ephesians 1:5** NLT

Once we boarded that plane, I knew nothing would ever be the same.

For starters, I never expected William would assimilate so quickly becoming a critic of airline food. He made his opinion well known during our first breakfast out of Africa just before we descended into Amsterdam.

"It this supposed to be a Rolex or something else?" he asked as he fumbled with the plastic casket containing the preformed egg tube and the spork utensil in shrink wrap.

In my mind I was thinking there would be many new and better breakfast experiences. Waffles with Syrup. French Toast with Cinnamon, Bacon with, more bacon. Yet the golden nugget to this whole story would become something entirely non-edible. The discovery was instead, something utterly biblical.

Sitting next to me on that plane was our new son. A young black man who looked nothing like me. His nose was different, hair completely dissimilar. He didn't speak like me, and wasn't remotely from the same place or culture. By all rights, he had no business being where he found himself, on a plane to the promised land at my side.

He wasn't a natural part of my blood family either, by a long shot. He had no business gathering around my daily breakfast, lunch or dinner tables. He was in this place solely of my wife's willing and reckless pursuit of love to go the distance. It was only because of this relentless commitment to her promise, and then our mutual willingness to fight for that covenant, that he was adopted into our family.

It's in fact, the same story of what God has done for each one of us. We're all adopted.

I closed my eyes and tried to get a little sleep, but I kept peeking to the person next to me, who was busy poking buttons on the moving screen, marveling at it all.

After 26 hours, our plane descended out of the Oregon clouds, the mighty Columbia River to our right, Mount Hood to our left. William had never seen snow before or a mountain from the sky either.

"Welcome to America!" I said when the plane's wheels touched the runway, perhaps a bit louder than I intended from my excitement and anticipation.

A few people seated around us whom, over the course of the last leg, had caught the gist of our story, applauded. They looked around their seat backs to catch a glimpse of William's first impressions and expressions.

"Pretty cool," he said.

At Customs, were processed in less than ten minutes. It was by far, the easiest part of the entire procedure. I was dumbfounded and overly delighted.

"Welcome to America," the agent said with a genuine smile. He put his hand out and firmly shook William's. "You've been given quite an opportunity, young man. Make the absolute best of it."

"Thank you sir, I will. It's good to finally be here."

After making our connection, it was exactly 3:16 p.m. when the wheels hit the ground at Eugene Airport. The timing was absolutely prophetic.

Through the large windows separating the tarmac from the terminal I caught an initial glimpse of more than a hundred people with balloons, signs and faces of anxious anticipation. Nearly the entire Three Sixteen church body, a good many friends, and a handful of relatives were all standing just outside of the security exit ropes.

Getting a step ahead of him and turning back on my camera I said, “Are you ready, William?”

He looked at me momentarily mystified but fully confident, like he was born for this moment. But just then, the waiting crowd caught the sight of his red, white and blue sweat top, and it sounded like we’d just entered a stadium with an Olympic medal winner.

The eruption of cheers was deafening as it blew out of the opened doors onto the tarmac catching most of the debarking passengers off guard.

“Oh my God,” I said. “Look at all these people.”

William took a deep breath and with his boyishly beautiful smile, absorbed it all, and with it, the hearts of everyone there.

Nita rushed at us first, nearly crossing the carpeted security line. Her face streamed with tears and was hysterically alive with joy. She cradled William’s face into her hands and gave him a long overdue kiss and hug. Then I got a “welcome-home-sailor-from-the-war” kind of smooches.

Behind her was Garrett and (his then girlfriend, now wife) Bethany; my daughter Mikayla and (her fiancé, now husband) Zack; along with Nita’s parents, Mary from California, and a throng of other friends and periphery folks too numerous to list.

Skirting across the whole line of people was a huge banner that read, "Welcome home William." Behind the sign, dozens of waving American flags, kids running around excitedly with red, white, and blue balloons, horns, ribbons. And more love than I'd ever seen in one place. Especially at an airport.

Hugs, kisses and jokes about how long my hair had gotten ensued. William disappeared in the midst of the commotion, working through the white-faced crowd. He liberally shook hands, hugged strangers and made easy conversation, as if he was running for mayor.

When the dizzying exhilaration had died down and the digital cameras took a break from recording the ecstatic homecoming, I looked around and couldn't find him.

With a voice of sudden concern I shouted, "Hey! Where's William?" To the laughs of the crowd, they opened up and he was standing in the center of the mob with his arms around total strangers and looking like he was loving all of the attention.

"Sheesh. I get him all the way home and lose him at the airport. What kind of an ending would that be?" I laughed, along with everyone else.

It was then my turn to say a few words of thanks.

"I want to thank you for all of you who didn't quit on us," I said, my voice breaking. "Regardless of what happens, what adversity, as long as we have God and each other, we will always win. I want you to remember that."

The entire airport seemingly broke out in applause. There were tears from strangers that followed my tears. It was almost too much to fathom.

The story had gotten that big. It affected those who were celebrating there at the airport all right, but even to all of those who had followed it on the margins. The tail end of the story even had an effect on the newcomers into it, those passengers just getting off the plane.

And that's how these kinds of stories filter and fall into the lives of those who never think they can do anything large and significant. Because God has adopted each one of us into his family, the work of His family is huge.

Everyone has a story. Everyone gets to have a significant part. The only requirement is, you just gotta show up when your name is called. And then you gotta say "yes." And mean it.

The rest will lead you to do hero work with a heart of humility, when you aren't busy trying to be a hero.

It won't be easy, but it will become the greatest story of your life. This is what delights God and fulfills that nagging hole of purpose that nothing else will fill.

The very next morning, William navigated down our carpeted stairs from his own bedroom in a brand new set of colorful PJ's. As he came down into the kitchen and sat down at the breakfast bar, that's when all of the dominos to this grand adventure lined up for me like biblical movie credits.

Nita and I had just lived through the tale of the human condition. We had just experienced, firsthand, a sampling of the adoption process mirrored by what God does for each one of us. How He fights profusely to keep his promise to bring us all back to His grand breakfast table by the grand plan, the Gospel of adoption.

It's where we each find ourselves undeservingly, unexpectedly and overwhelmingly in His house, in His presence getting all the privileges, including eating His food, enjoying the bounty. We belong to a family. We get our own room. This is the very story of the Gospel.

That morning, William Biyinzika Loveall sat at my breakfast table. Fully adopted in, and fully fought for through all of the obstacles. He stole our hearts. He was worth the effort.

"You're home now William," I said. "Now how about some bacon?"

I get to live this Gospel message every morning… because the Gospel sits at my breakfast table.

EPILOGUE

William is fully and legally our son now. He has an Oregon birth certificate, a U.S. passport and he has a paragraph in our will as an heir. He has full rights and benefits of our family name as a son.

William finished the seventh grade that Spring he arrived. Again, for the third time. It's now a joke around our house. "Three of the best years of William's life were in the seventh grade." Ha, ha.

His first day of class, he arrived at school to a standing ovation of classmates who had been praying for him the whole time we were in Africa. Once he walked into the classroom, he fit right into the middle school life like he was born to be there.

The following winter of his eighth grade year, he played his first basketball season, helping his team win the district championship. He ran track for the first time, setting school records in the relay and the 400 meters.

Pizza and hamburgers have naturally become some of his favorite foods. But nothing tops a burrito. He wasn't as impressed with Costco hot dogs as I would have hoped. Bacon brings a special kind of grin to his face still to this day.

In the past three years of being here, he has learned that being in a family takes sacrifices from everyone. Like most teen-age kids, it's a learned realization that the world doesn't always revolve around him. I want, means in our house that you will work, and he's learning how to steward money. Well, at least he's still learning the ins and outs of that concept.

Nita and I have said many times that, "teenagers are global," meaning they all have those common idiosyncrasies that all of us have lived and parented through.

During a time of intense fellowship, over a lesson about entitlement, we considered emptying his room of everything, including his bed. The "have everything" lifestyle was seeping its way into William's expectations as he was complaining about his basic mobile phone and the fact that we don't have cable TV.

Even though he was just a year out of Africa, the memory and appreciation of where he had come from was disappearing too soon. At one point, Nita and I felt we weren't making that deep family connection we had hoped for. So we took him to his favorite Mexican dinner place and asked him straight up, what he thought love was.

"It's when people give you things," he said resolutely. "You are my parents, you are suppose to give me the things I want. When people came to the orphanage, they brought us things and that meant that they loved us."

So as you might imagine, we too, had a lot to learn in the continuing family processes. We didn't end up taking his bed out of his room and we all learned a thing or two about love, gratitude and appreciation for what we do have—each other. We learned to adopt new ways of showing the unique ways each one receives love so it is expressed in a way we can readily see it. FYI William, love isn't cable TV or video games or an Iphone. Good thing, cause we ain't getting any of them in the very near future.

His second summer included a trip to California's Huntington Beach. I will never forget the observation from the pier he made while looking out at the breaker water. There were dozens of people dressed in black wetsuits waiting to catch waves.

"Hey dad, why is it that only black people surf?"

"Those are like insulated shirts that keep everyone warm…white people included." I laughed.

I've been telling him since he got here that his story of faith will be a large part of his eventual ministry. But like most teenagers, he's slipped into the belief that it's not worth telling for fear of not fitting in. William fits in. He wears Nike socks, brightly colored shirts, and sports either a big Afro hairdo or corn-rowed shoulder-length braids. Kids love him. He was elected to Freshman and Sophomore student council and took the best looking girl to his first homecoming. Come on, it doesn't get much better than that.

On his first mission trip to Mexico during Spring Break he was sharing around the campfire one evening. Starting from the first vision through the last hurdle with the airport customs official, he shared the entire faith experience of how he arrived into America and into our family. The host mother, a high school teacher, was so moved by the story that she asked to borrow William to have him speak at the next day's classes. He shared his testimony to four different groups of kids and when he came back to our home town, he was asked to share it again in front of a mega-church gathering of all of the youth kids' parents. Microphones, rolling camera's, spotlights.

"I felt for the first time while in Mexico that I actually had something to share, instead of being someone receiving what someone was sharing with me," he said. "I also realized that my journey of faith can be used to inspire people to believe in what God reveals to them and to trust the process."

The end of his freshman year, Will (that's what the kids call him) finished with a 3.60 GPA. That's significant because he attends a private, college prep high school. He also received a varsity letter in both soccer and track. And our favorite Mexican restaurant gave him a job dressing up as a taco and waving a sign on the sidewalk for a few hours a week. He likes the job. He hates paying the chunk for taxes. He recently got promoted to bus boy and loves making tips for hard work.

He's saved nearly enough to buy his first car and started off-street driving instruction in the local church parking lot after getting his permit.

After the Oregon Ducks made it to the National Football Championships, William wanted to try out for football. He made it through the first week of drills but when he was running receiver routes, tore an ACL.

Come to find out, he had done that when he was about 10 playing a pick-up soccer game in Uganda. According to William the village lady massaged his knee and after a few weeks, he was able to walk on it.

He's recovered now fully and is looking forward. Forward to track. Forward to college. Forward to anything he puts his mind and efforts to.

Oh, and he finally got an Iphone…

Welcome home, kid. You're doing awesome.

ACKNOWLEDGEMENTS

There are many famous author quotes I carry with me, "Writing is the art of re-writing." and "I hate to write but I love to have written," are just a few.

It took nearly 20 months to bring The Gospel Sits at My Breakfast Table together. Time keeps everything from happening all at once, especially when I was trying to rush the finish. The extended time brought the "A" team to help make this book it's best.

Bob Welch, one of my most favorite writers in the whole world agreed during a break in his book schedule to "do the full deal" on it. My period and comma people, Steven Schmidt and Stephanie Hoffman, found hidden mistakes and typos that were buried deep. The gritty cover and graphics were the vision of Bethany Loveall, who is my favorite daughter-in-law. The encouragement of my kids, Garrett and Mikayla, and her husband Zach, and many friends were invaluable. Plus the convenient loss of employment made the time available to get it done. I thank God that I couldn't stop the words from coming out while He provided the needs during the process. And of course, to William, whose prayer and faith shaped a story larger than life itself.

And lastly, to my beloved wife, who was critical, helpful, loving and wholly dedicated to see this entire story through with me to the end…besides, she's the one who got us into this mess in the first place.

And from Nita: A special *thank you* to Mary, whom I wanted you to know that our 30-plus-year friendship has been one of the greatest gifts of my life. That week you dropped everything and came to Oregon, got me through one of the most emotionally demanding stretches of stress and fragile emotions of my life. My sincerest "Thank You" is a mere shadow of my immense gratitude for that gesture of love and support.

54028876R00143

Made in the USA
Charleston, SC
22 March 2016